IF THE 60s WERE THE 90s

IF THE 60s WERE THE 90s

An Ode to Venice Beach

Michael Ruark

SPRING CEDARS

This work depicts actual events in the life of the author as truthfully as recollection permits. While all persons within are actual individuals, some names and identifying characteristics have been changed to respect their privacy.

First edition, 2023

Cover artwork by Lauren Zurcher
Book design by Spring Cedars

ISBN 978-1-950484-53-9 (paperback)
ISBN 978-1-950484-54-6 (ebook)

Published by Spring Cedars
Denver, Colorado
www.springcedars.com

Table of Contents

My Nightmare

A lady stands speaking in tongues, just loud enough so that all other sounds stop. This is a regular event on Sundays at the small Texas church; only twenty-five people sit in the congregation. After the lady stops speaking, there is a long pause, no one makes the slightest move. All breathing becomes quiet, all eyes are closed and waiting in a bubble of darkness.

The preacher of the church slowly rises from his seat at the front chancel. He walks to the pulpit, and after another short moment of silence, he begins, "Oh my people, this is the Lord thy God, you have pleased me with your virtue and righteousness. The day of my coming is at hand. We shall sit together in the heights of Heaven. The path of goodness is in your heart; with love and kindness all greatness is possible. You are my people. I am with you always. My chastisement will shine on the day of judgment. Everything hidden in the darkness will be shown in the light. This is the Lord thy God." Again, there is a long pause. Then the preacher lifts his arms and says, "God has been with us. We are on holy ground." The congregation erupts into praise. A few people rush to the altar. Surely, the Lord has been here today.

A boy of seven years old sits in the congregation, his forehead pressed to the pew, frozen in stillness and shallow half-breathing, not to make any sound or movement. The thoughts race through his young mind. Is the preacher blessed by God? Are the words direct from God? It must be so, right? Is this man speaking for God, a loving God and a vengeful God? A God that will hurt you if you do wrong. A God that will turn you into a pillar of salt if you let your eyes wander. He questions, never could he go against such certainty, right?

***

The next scene flashes to this same preacher hitting his wife in the face and grabbing her by the hair. He is trying to give her uppercut blows; a grown man hitting a woman as if she were a man, like a heavyweight fighter against a featherweight. The preacher and his family are at a motel for the night, on their way to Bible college in North Dakota. They have driven all day and into the night and are very tired. After passing so many No Vacancy signs, they had finally found a motel with a vacant room.

In his rage, the preacher throws his wife to the ground and grabs her by the throat. Sitting on her chest, he has both hands securely wrapped around her neck. Surely, this time, he will kill her. She gasps and fights for her last breath, her face begins to turn blue as life is slipping from her body. In her mind, she desperately pleads, "Will someone please save me, will someone stop this evil?"

Three children, an older daughter and two sons, stand off to the side and watch the horror. As the tragedy unfolds, they struggle to understand why this has become their norm. How can Dad be doing this? Isn't he the preacher that speaks as God? Isn't he the prophet that understands what God wants? How can he be killing our mom, in front of us? Panic rushes through their hearts, and despair overcomes their reason.

All of a sudden, the seven-year-old middle son breaks through his shock and rushes toward the preacher. Out of fear and preservation for their sibling's welfare, the older sister and younger brother grab the boy's arms and try to hold him back. He breaks free and jumps on the preacher's back. This snaps the preacher out of his trance of rage, and he lets go of their mom's throat. He turns and punches the boy in the face, again and again. Throughout this beating, the boy thinks, at least Mom is alive; and now I am a man, and my father hates me, forever.

The preacher screams and tells his family to go to sleep. He continues to walk around the room as if stalking his prey. The young boy tries to go to sleep as quickly as he can; he keeps his eyes shut tight, without a flinch, once again in that bubble of darkness. Without signal, he is brutally hoisted out of bed and accused of fake sleeping by the preacher. The preacher punches the boy in the face as the scene fades to black.

***

This was my nightmare. But it was real, all real. I grew up in a fundamentalist Pentecostal environment. Religious fundamentalists believe in the superiority of their religious teachings, and the strict division between righteous people and evildoers. So we never went to movies, carnivals, or circuses; My mom and my sister couldn't wear make-up or pants. The church and the preacher were the ultimate authority. My father was supposed to be a righteous man, yet he lived in hypocrisy. How could you speak in the name of God and have rage in your heart? How could you abuse the ones that love you? This so-called preacher was from an Old Testament ideal of beating others into submission. He would stand at the pulpit and speak of love and Jesus, of how we should all be good people and show compassion to one another. It was a lie. He did not show compassion; he was moved by anger and non-love. I despised him; he was a fraud, a cheat, and a sorry excuse for a man. I had been made to become a mad dog, and still a beaten dog. At twenty-seven years old, I had become a bitter alcoholic, someone I didn't even know. I had to try and find a way to flee from any thought of my father, his hypocritical religion, and this fear of God. I had to run far away from Denver. And so I did, into the arms of Venice Beach.

Sleeping In My Traveling Home

A ray of sunlight peeks through a small uncovered hole in the car window; it shines on my face, waking me from this deep-rooted nightmare of my father hitting me and my family. When will these moments of my childhood let me forget? As always, these memories are a constant nuisance as I begin another day. I look around the backseat to make sure everything is okay, I quickly check the front seat, another night of safety. This 1963 Chrysler 300 is the best investment I ever made. *I bought the car for $500 from a bartender at an old bakery restaurant in Dogtown, where I used to work. The guy who sold it to me was really cool, a real California skater. He always had his skateboard with him. He even knew Tony Hawk, they grew up together.* My car is a traveling home. I can sleep in the backseat with privacy by hanging two suit jackets in the windows and a towel draped over the middle bar on the inside roof. A regular paradise. At least I am in Los Angeles; I'm not asking anyone for anything. I am homeless and self-sufficient.

I get out of the car and grab the water I keep in the trunk to wash my face, brush my teeth, comb my hair, and some days, shave. I grab one of my waiter shirts, iron it on the front seat, along with my pants. People pass by and look at me with mystery, like Detective Columbo is looking at you. I try to be as inconspicuous as possible. I do not want anyone knowing I am sleeping in my car. After cleaning up, I sometimes drive to a friend's apartment. It is one of those apartment floors that has a common bathroom in the hall.

She lets me use the bathroom to take a shower and get more cleaned up. Then, I am off to work. I work two jobs and am still living in my car.

***

I work at a Chinese restaurant on Santa Monica Boulevard during the day. I wait tables on the lunch shift and am the only employee who was born in the USA. It is a challenge. Often, when I walk up to large tables with about ten to fifteen Chinese customers, they look at me thinking it is a joke—a couple of instances they request another waiter. The customers and other employees can at times be hard on me; I take it and keep working. I greet the tables in Chinese and provide great service, which results in real good tips. The only other waiter that is not from China is from Morocco. He speaks good English, we get along well.

I was hired at this restaurant by a younger Chinese guy named Kenny. His father in China owns the restaurant, while he manages it. Kenny is very cool. Each day, he learns more English and American ways by talking to me, and I learn to speak a little Chinese and grow to love Chinese culture. It is a great arrangement for me to work there. At the end of each lunch shift, the cooks prepare a big meal, all the staff sit together at the same table and eat the best Chinese food in the world, real original stuff. I love it. Also, this meal never costs me anything, I appreciate that. After eating, I generally have a couple of hours to waste before my next job. I drive somewhere, park, and sit in my car. I read a book or listen to the radio. When someone doesn't have a home, boredom is a constant annoyance.

At 5:30 pm, I go to work at another restaurant in Santa Monica, right off of Wilshire Boulevard, called Michael's Santa Monica, located at 1147 Third Street. A really nice place, very upscale. It opened in 1979 and is credited as an early pioneer of farm-to-table California cuisine utilizing local produce and hyper-seasonal ingredients. There is also a Michael's New York in midtown Manhattan. Many top Hollywood stars dine at Michael's. I have delivered food to the tables of Dustin Hoffman and Julia Roberts. Some nights there can be about 250 guests in the restaurant.

I am not a waiter at Michael's. I am a food runner, running three plates of food from the kitchen to the tables. We offer American fine dining, serving from the left, clearing from the right, and decrumbing the table. The plates coming out of the kitchen are so hot, I once burn the inside of my arm, but it just has to continue burning while I serve. Michael's provides uniforms for the night shift, no laundry or ironing necessary. The uniforms were designed years earlier by Ralph Lauren. Most of my shifts are spent supporting a great waiter named Ethan. He is very cool, so patient, a true professional. I want to do my best to make his customers happy, and we work well together. At the end of the night, Michael's lets the staff get a discounted meal. We always eat awesome food.

After my shift, I sometimes stick around and talk with a few of the Mexican cooks, maybe get a six-pack or smoke some mota. These cooks are fun to hang out with, they give me shit the whole time. Pinche Gringo this, Pinche Gringo that; it is all in good fun. I pick up Spanish cuss words quickly and learn to talk shit back to them in Spanish. They like it. Then, I hop in my car to find a safe neighborhood in Santa Monica to park and sleep. A lot of times, I park by Goose Egg Park. Some nights, I have to drive around for at least an hour to find just the right spot. No one at either restaurant knows I am sleeping in my car. Day after day, I have this same routine. Time seems to stand still. Yet, with all this activity, I still cannot get enough money for the first month's rent and security deposit.

***

On my days off, I go all around Santa Monica. I take walks in the mile-and-a-half long Palisades Park on Ocean Avenue by the ends of Broadway, Santa Monica Boulevard, Arizona Avenue, and Wilshire Boulevard, gazing at the beautiful Santa Monica Bay. It's strange how sometimes when you look out at the ocean it seems like the ocean is taller than the land. Kind of looks like a big wave. A little spooky when you first see it. I take walks down to Santa Monica Beach and dip my feet in the water, sometimes dive in and swim.

Or I walk the Santa Monica Stairs on the "secret Mesa stairway", which has the most steps and is used less. I walk on the 3rd Street Promenade, an outdoor, pedestrian-only shopping district that stretches for three blocks between Broadway and Wilshire Boulevard. Along the promenade there are usually a few street performers. It is also nice to visit Santa Monica Place, a three-level outdoor shopping mall, at the Promenade's southern end; I get some lunch at the food court and go to the third-floor rooftop deck for a view of the Pacific Ocean. There is also a great pool hall on the promenade called Yankee Doodles that I go to at 1410 3rd Street Promenade, they have 29 tables.

Sometimes, I walk to the Santa Monica Pier and hang out. It is a large, double-jointed pier at the foot of Colorado Avenue. Half of the pier was built in 1909 and the second half in 1916. It is great to pass under the iconic, arched blue sign that reads, "Santa Monica Yacht Harbor – Sport Fishing – Boating – Cafes," unveiled on June 17, 1941. I also like to visit the Pacific Park, which is the West Coast's only amusement park located on a pier. One time, I rode the Looff Hippodrome Carousel which was built in 1922 and was where Paul Newman worked in the 1973 movie *The Sting*. There is also a sign at the end of the Santa Monica Pier that marks the end of the old Route 66 highway; a primary route for those who migrated west between 1929 and 1939 during the Great Depression. This pier is always crowded with people having a great time.

Another one of my favorite things to do is to ride my bike up the Marvin Braude Bike Trail from Santa Monica Beach to Will Rogers Beach in Pacific Palisades. It is about a three-mile ride each way. This coastal bike path is the most popular paved bike path in Los Angeles County with great views of the Pacific Ocean. On a clear day, I can see Catalina Island on the horizon. Some days, I hang out in Temescal Canyon. There is a nice three-mile trail that goes through the canyon. It takes about two hours and is one of LA's greatest hikes with amazing views of Malibu, the Santa Monica mountains, and Downtown. You go up to 1,190 feet above sea level, and on a clear day you can see from the San Gabriel Mountains to Catalina. The trail begins and ends in Temescal Gateway Park at 15601 Sunset Boulevard in Pacific Palisades. Some of the buildings at the entrance were built in 1922.

***

Today, I am off to see the movie *The Doors* directed by Oliver Stone. I am not a huge fan of The Doors, but I do want to see every movie Oliver Stone has directed. Besides, Jim Morrison is a California icon; I have to see it. I am going with a couple girls I know. I tell them if the movie is good, I have a joint in my pocket, and I am going to spark it up right in the theater. They tell me I wouldn't do it. Well, about a third of the way through the movie, I can't wait any longer. I pull out the joint and start to light it. The girls tell me to stop, they don't want smoke around us. They're scared. So, I walk down to the second row by myself and smoke it alone. *That day, Jim Morrison kind of leapt into my psyche.*

***

A few days later, I am walking in Palisades Park at the end of Wilshire Boulevard when a local news camera crew rushes up to me. "What do you think of the Rodney King incident?"

A quick recap of the incident they are asking about: On March 3, 1991, the California Highway Patrol pulled over a speeding motorist, Rodney King. He had been drinking earlier and admitted that he did try to dodge the police, but he eventually pulled his car over in front of an apartment building. The CHP were then joined by the LAPD. A resident of the apartment building woke up to the commotion outside. He grabbed his camcorder and recorded a video of four police officers brutally kicking and beating King after he had fallen to the ground.

I answer the news crew, "I think it is a tragedy. The cops were beating him down, and he wasn't even trying to get up, yet they just kept beating him. That has happened forever, though, cops beating people. They were definitely beating Rodney King because he was Black, that's for sure. They had no idea they were being filmed. When they took Rodney King to the hospital, he had a broken right ankle, multiple fractured facial bones, bruises all over his body, and burns on his chest where they repeatedly used a 50,000-volt stun gun. Racism in America has been around forever; until the USA admits that racism is still around, and apologizes for its corrupt past, this country will never achieve its full potential."

The crew breaks into big smiles. "That was great. Wonderful, just loved it. Now, do you think you can say it again one more time, exactly like you just did?"

I remember thinking, what the hell, this isn't a joke, I'm not an actor. Did they even have any idea what I just said? "Fine, let's do it again." LA was like that, I was starting to learn; anything could happen. At least the climate was warm, and the scenery was beautiful.

***

Eventually, I start to broaden my places to visit. One day, I go to Rodeo Drive, ranked the fourth most-visited destination in the Los Angeles area; I visit Two Rodeo Drive, the coolest outdoor shopping center I have ever seen, located in Beverly Hills on the corner of Wilshire Boulevard and Rodeo Drive, across from the Beverly Wilshire Hotel. Of course, I am just window shopping. Two Rodeo Drive was sold in 1991 for $1,500 per square foot, the highest reported price per square foot of any commercial real estate at that time in the history of the USA.

I also drive up Highway 1, the most iconic roadway in California, called the Pacific Coast Highway. I drive to Malibu, or stop at Topanga Beach; I like to hang out there. One day, I splurge and go to the Chart House at 18412 Pacific Coast Highway for a late lunch. Sometimes, I go up to Corral Canyon and take a hike. One of my favorite drives is to take Highway 27 from PCH to Topanga. It is such a remote drive, no houses or people. There is about a 3-mile stretch that reminds me of Colorado. It is like being in the mountains in LA.

Today, I am parked on the side of the highway in Malibu by Ratner Beach and the Villa de Leon mansion built in 1926, just admiring the ocean, and the most beautiful girl I have ever seen comes walking up to my car.

She says, "Hey, how are you doing?"

I shyly reply, "Oh, I'm doing good, just checking out the ocean."

She leans into my window, and we talk for about five minutes. What a California babe, she smells so good, it must be the suntan lotion.

"Hey, do you think you can drive me up to Tongva Park? It's right by the Santa Monica Pier, I'm supposed to meet my friends there, and I'm already late."

"Sure, hop in." Anything for a beautiful girl.

***

I keep hearing about this crazy Venice Beach. It is supposed to be wild. Everybody I know tells me it is too dangerous.

"Don't go down there, you'll get robbed," they say.

How bad can it be when 10 million people visit annually? The Venice Beach Boardwalk is the second most popular attraction in Los Angeles, second only to Disneyland. I have to visit.

So, I go to the Venice Beach Boardwalk, also known as Ocean Front Walk; a two-and-a-half mile, pedestrian-only promenade. Most of the funky shops and cafes are on a one-mile section between Rose Avenue in the north and North Venice Boulevard in the south. I spend the whole Sunday just soaking in wonderful California. I have lunch and walk around watching everything and everyone. It's fascinating, all the different people: artists, singers, tarot card readers, fortune tellers, a guy walking on glass, sword swallowers, comedians, jewelers, portrait painters, someone juggling chainsaws, a crowd of moving Hare Krishnas, real hippie stuff. I learn that street artists who perform entertainment for donations are called buskers. Some of the most beautiful girls in the world pass by me, I'm in awe, all the bikinis. A few times I muster the nerve to talk to them.

I have read that most of the visitors to Venice are between the ages of 25 and 34. On Sundays, there can be more than 100,000 people on the boardwalk. In 1991, Venice actually beat out Disneyland in terms of tourist numbers. This is much different than Santa Monica. A lot more action here. I'm beginning to really like it. Venice Beach is a young man's paradise.

***

A little history on the area: Venice's founder, Abbot Kinney, was born on a farm near New Brunswick, New Jersey on November 16, 1850. In 1874, Abbot was made a partner in his older brothers' tobacco business. Their most popular brand of hand-rolled cigarettes was Sweet Caporal. After Kinney built his summer home in Santa Monica in 1886, he became interested in land development along the Pacific Coast. In 1891, Kinney and another partner bought controlling interest in the Ocean Park Casino and that same year, purchased the surrounding tract of land that faced the ocean south of Santa Monica, 1.5 miles long and 1,000 feet deep. The property curved eastward to a depth of half a mile along the southern end. The northern third, located in Santa Monica, had development potential, while the remaining county territory was wetlands consisting of sand dunes and marsh. They began building roads, homes, and parks, and officially named the area Ocean Park in May 1895. On June 30, 1898, Santa Monica granted Kinney permission to build a pier. In 1902, Abbot Kinney and his partners decided to dissolve their company and divide the property on a coin toss. Kinney, who won the toss, surprisingly chose the marshy, undeveloped southern half to build his new grand resort, Venice of America, a recreation of Venice, Italy, on the shores of the Pacific.

On July 4, 1905, Venice of America officially opened. The resort included 16 miles of canals with gondolas and singing gondoliers; a 1,200-foot-long pier with the Venice Dancing Pavilion, a bowling alley, a Casino, a Bandstand Tower, the Ship Cafe, the Ship Hotel Cabrillo, which was permanently on piles beside the pier, the Big Dipper Roller Coaster, a 3,000-seat auditorium called the Venetian Gardens, a heated, salt-water pool that could accommodate 2,000 bathers called the Venice Plunge, an Aquarium which exhibited the finest collection of marine specimens on the Pacific Coast in 48 glass tanks; 190 resort cottages; several commercial buildings, police and fire stations; a miniature steam railroad ran on a 3-mile track around the entire park; and a 60-foot long breakwater to protect the facilities. Soon Venice was established as the "Coney Island of California."

Venice's founder moved his family to 16 Park Avenue in Venice in 1905. His wife and children lived there until she died in 1914. His son, Sherwood, lived there in the 1920's. In 1911, Venice was disincorporated from Ocean Park, which remained part of Santa Monica. In 1920, on November 4, Abbot Kinney died. On December 20, the Abbot Kinney Pier burned down. The Venice Pier business was carried on by Kinney's oldest son, Thornton. A new pier was built and opened on May 28, 1921. Venice was annexed to Los Angeles on November 25, 1925, and due to blue laws and various licensing restrictions, business started to drastically slow. By 1929, Los Angeles had filled in and paved over the lagoon and most of the canals. In 1930, oil was discovered in Venice; within a year, 148 oil wells were producing over 40,000 barrels of oil daily; oil production ended in Venice by 1932. The Venice pier closed on April 20, 1946, because Los Angeles refused to renew the Kinney Company's tidelands lease. In 1950, the Kinney Company's Venice Pier beach property was sold to the State of California for $640,000.

Due to the long-term negligent attitude toward the area in the 1950's and early 1960's, Venice became known as "The Ghetto by the Sea." In 1958, the pier became part of a 28-acre nautical-themed park to compete with Disneyland. In 1964, 550 historic buildings in downtown Venice and along the beach were demolished; LA even had plans to tear down all of Venice's 1600 buildings. Los Angeles waged a war to evict the "undesirables" from the community, especially in the Black Oakwood neighborhood, curiously by leaving that area for the last phase of the demolition project, the Oakwood community had the extra time to organize against code enforcement to remain intact. In the summer of 1967, the first of the Hippie invasions of Flower Children happened. In 1974, nude sunbathing was permitted for a short while. In 1977, Venice regained popularity as the "Roller Skating Capital of the World." Today, Venice is a small beach community with a population of 41,000 people, covering only 3.1 square miles; bordered by the Pacific Ocean to the southwest, Marina del Rey to the southeast, Culver City to the east, Mar Vista to the northeast, and Santa Monica to the north.

***

I occasionally drive down to the southern part of Venice Beach, at the end of West Washington Boulevard. In this area is the Venice Fishing Pier, a 1,310-foot concrete structure originally built in 1965. This pier suffered damage in 1983. *As long as I lived in Venice, this pier was closed to the public.* I often get some crispy calamari at the Venice Whaler, at 10 Washington Boulevard, which has been there since 1944; also a favorite watering hole to the Doors, Beatles, and Beach Boys. Down the street is 11 Anchorage Street, nicknamed The Castle; Francis Bushman the silent screen star built the stone structure in 1922, and was frequently visited by Rudolph Valentino. A couple of blocks north is The Venice Beach House at 15 30th Avenue; a boutique hotel built in 1911, featuring nine suites and gardens referred to as "The Oasis of Venice Beach." There is a great pool hall at 15 Washington Boulevard called Hinano Cafe, there since 1962. It was Jim Morrison's favorite Venice hangout. I play pool there for hours. I win a lot, and the place has some really good shooters.

One day, this old man comes up to me and asks, "Hey, would you like to play?"

"Sure. You ain't no shark are you?"

He smiles. "No, but I bet you are."

We play pool for about four hours, game after game. He's good. He beats me a bunch of times. But I win more than he does.

The old man asks, "Do you live in Venice?"

"Yes."

"Oh okay, I have a house in Playa Vista. Where do you live? "

"Well, if you really want to know, I sleep in my car."

"Really, what do you do for a living?"

"I wait tables at a couple of restaurants."

We talk for a while longer, and then I leave. A few days later, I go back to play more pool, and there he is. We start shooting again and wager a-beer-a-game.

After about an hour, he says, "Hey, I have a sailboat at Marina Del Rey. I only use it when I'm sailing. Would you like to sleep on the boat?"

"Sure. That'd be great."

So, he takes me to the harbor and shows me the boat. It is small, maybe a 20-footer, but it's cool, and at least it will be safe. I start spending my nights on the boat in the Marina Del Rey harbor; it is North America's largest man-made, small-craft harbor, completed in 1962, and home to 4,100 boats and 22 marinas and anchorages.

After about a week, the old man comes by just to check up on me. "Hey, tomorrow morning I'm going sailing. Would you like to join me?"

"Yeah, sure. I've only been sailing once, back in Colorado at Lake Dillon up in the mountains. Never in the ocean, though. That would be cool."

The next day, we sail out of the harbor into the Pacific Ocean. The boat is going up and down on the waves so much I have to hold on for dear life. It's scary being out in all this water. My mom was scared of water when I was growing up, so even though I can swim great, I am a little afraid of the water myself. My dad almost drowned me, teaching me to swim. It is a great experience, though, to sail on the ocean.

When we get back to the marina, the old man is acting kind of differently. He tries to sit all close to me. I wonder if the dude is gay. It makes me feel uncomfortable. "Hey, man, I'm not gay," I say.

This upsets him, and he tells me that he isn't gay either. We start arguing.

Finally, I just say, "I'm out of here. I won't be staying on your boat anymore. Thank you."

***

After visiting Venice a few times, I walk to the north part of the boardwalk, by the end of Dudley Avenue and Rose Avenue. I am looking for someone to buy weed from, and I see this dark-skinned Black dude sitting on a bench. He seems like a real tough guy, kind of scary. He has very short little dreads. This guy knows where the weed is, I think, so I casually walk up and sit on the bench beside him. He doesn't even look at me.

After sitting there for a couple of minutes, I say, "Hey, how are you doing?"

"Good, just trying to enjoy the day."

"Cool. It's a beautiful day. So, are you from Venice?"

"No, I'm from Miami. But I stay down here most of the time now. Where are you from?"

"I am from Denver. In Colorado. I have been in LA for about three months."

"Colorado, that's a really nice place, I hear. A lot of

mountains, right?"

"Yeah. Did you know that there are 96 mountains in the United States that are over 14,000 feet tall, and Colorado has more than half of them? Colorado has 53, Alaska has 29. Colorado is called God's Country."

"Why did you leave and come to California?"

"Oh, I have a script that I am going to show to Oliver Stone, see if he likes it."

"Wow, that's cool. Did you write it all yourself?"

"Yeah."

"What's it about?"

"It's about a guy that crosses the country on a motorcycle, an Indian motorcycle. A kind of rock opera, a lot of music and just a little dialogue. It starts out in downtown Chicago in the Sears Tower as a black and white silent movie; then it slowly turns into a color movie with the song *Voodoo Child*, the Stevie Ray Vaughan version. The guy rides down I-55 to New Orleans, where he meets up with this other guy with a motorcycle who saves his life. Then they ride to California, together, stopping along the way at a bunch of places, like Mesa Verde and Las Vegas. It ends in South Central. There is also an angel that appears all along the way."

"Damn, that sounds pretty good."

"Thank you. Hey, my name is Mike. What's yours?"

"Bruce. I'm the King of Miami. Nice to meet you."

"You, too. King of Miami, what's that all about?"

"I used to run Miami; it was my town. The entire town was mine. I ran the whole thing."

"Why did you leave?"

"I had to get out of town, because of some old issues."

As long as I knew Bruce, he never explained the issues that wouldn't let him return to Miami to be the King.

"So, what do you do for work?" Bruce asks.

"Oh, I work at a couple of restaurants in Santa Monica. I'm a waiter at one and a food runner at another."

"Really, what kind of food?"

"Chinese food in the day and California cuisine at night at a place called Michael's. It's one of the best restaurants in Santa Monica. Have you ever heard of it?"

"No. Well, that's cool you got work."

"What do you do?"

"I don't have a job right now. I'm sleeping on the ground. I just try to spread my hustle any way I can."

Over time, I understood that was one of Bruce's favorite things to say: spread your hustle this, spread your hustle that. Always, spread your hustle. He worked too hard at being himself.

"Wow, I just love Venice Beach. It's so cool down here. It's as if the 60s were the 90s," I say.

"Yeah, it's always a wild time on the boardwalk. Have you seen Harry Perry playing guitar on roller skates?"

"No, I haven't. There's just so much to see, shit, it seems like there's never a dull moment. Pretty exciting." We talk for about ten minutes. Then I ask, "Hey, do you know where I can get some weed around here?"

"You want weed, no problem. I can get you weed. Hey, you ain't no cop, are you?"

"No, I'm not a cop. Hell, does a cop have this long of hair?"

"You sure you ain't a cop?"

"Yes, I'm sure."

"Okay, well how much do you need?"

"Oh, about $20 worth."

"Okay, give me the money, I need to walk over to a place and get it."

"Man, I ain't giving you the money; you're gonna rip me off."

"No, Mike, I'm not gonna rip you off. I just don't have it here with me."

"Are you sure you won't fuck me over?"

"No, Mike, I won't."

So I give him the $20, and he disappears. To my surprise, in less than five minutes, he walks back and says he has what I want. *I think that was what actually established my initial trust in Bruce.* "Hey, you want to go walk somewhere and have a smoke?" I ask.

"Okay, we can go out by the water. The cops don't go out there."

Bruce was my first friend in Venice. He showed me the way; he introduced me to the other homeless people on the beach. It was also nice to have someone to buy weed from, making things real easy. Bruce was one of those guys who always had a way of talking just a little too loud. He didn't mean anything by it, I guess; it was just his natural way. He had no concept of other people and was not the least bit shy of jumping in someone's face and starting an argument. He was pretty trustworthy, just a little shady, you had to watch your back with him. He also thought he was a philosopher, always talking, never silent. To hear him talk, he knew more than almost everyone else in the world and was the born leader in any given situation. In the beginning, Bruce was a great friend and a brother to me. He just would never shut the fuck up. I guess he was a little bit of a gangster, just not OG. He was a street hood, yet there still was a bit of a snobbish air about him; he seemed undaunted by his surroundings and anyone in them. I guess that was why he called himself the King of Miami. Even though he wasn't in Miami.

***

Tonight, I sit in my car thinking, wow, I am truly free. I have two jobs, and I'm making some money; and I get to take little vacations on my days off. I am making friends in LA on my own. I am a man, I am strong. All those things that were told to me in my youth are not true. I am not a failure, I am not bad. I am not like my father. I do not need someone to tell me I am whole. I don't need anything. I can love God in my own way, I don't need any religion to show me how.

It was a magical time. Sometimes, even at the bottom, there was hope. I had hope. Funny, it didn't seem like the bottom to me, this was freedom. I always knew at the core of my soul I had value, lies cannot take away the days of my life. If you are a good person, then you are; if you aren't, then you aren't. That seemed simple at the time, sitting in my car, and even today. One time, I heard someone say they didn't trust prosperity. I think it was in the movie Tender Mercies. Well, I didn't believe that then, or now. Time is to be; we just get to live it.

On that note though of not trusting prosperity, first, I get fired from the Chinese restaurant. A new restaurant manager is appointed. He is an older man from Shanghai, I'll say in his early fifties. When we first meet, he immediately doesn't like me. He is one of those guys who lives in America and still has an unfavorable view of the people and the country. Always complaining.

I think it surprises most Americans that the USA isn't universally admired and regarded as the greatest nation on Earth; and that our democracy is not the only form of democracy out there. Not everybody sees America as a shining city on a hill. Though most would like to live here, I think.

The new manager often complains to Kenny about me, "Why do we have this guy waiting tables in our restaurant? He is an American and can't speak Chinese, let's get rid of him."

Kenny stands up for me, "No, we are going to keep him; he is good for the restaurant."

So the new manager bears down on me, "Do your prep work better. Run the food faster. Learn more Chinese." He will never be satisfied until I am gone.

Eventually, Kenny travels back to China to visit his father for a full month. That is just the opportunity the manager is looking for. I come into work, and he immediately asks, "Why isn't your shirt ironed?"

"I ironed it this morning."

"No, you didn't."

Later that day, after my shift, he pulls me aside and says, "Michael, we no longer need your services. We're cutting back and must let you go."

They aren't cutting back, I know that's a lie. Every day the lunch crowd is packed. I have to run my ass off just trying to keep up.

Well, one job down. I have my daytime hours off now.

What can I do to fill the time? I start to think about doing some art on Venice Beach. There are artists on the boardwalk that don't seem that great; how could I be any worse? It seems they are making money. Maybe I can do some writing. I have been writing for about five years and have at least five hundred pages of writing in my trunk. Before I came to LA, I used to sit in my room in Colorado and write for hours; I'd write poetry, short stories, slogans, all kinds of stuff. I can write anything. So, I will write poetry on the boardwalk.

***

Whenever I visit Venice, I park my Chrysler in the Rose Avenue parking lot, right by the beach. Today is no different. I park and make my way down the boardwalk. I go into the Candle Cafe at 325 Ocean Front Walk and order a beer. I'm sitting outside on the patio, and up walks Bruce.

"What's up, Mike?"

"Hey, Bruce, how are you doing today? Have a seat. Where's the bud?"

"Oh, I got some if you need some."

"Okay, cool. Hey, you want a beer?" I ask.

"Sure, Mike."

As Bruce and I watch the girls go by and have a few cold ones, Harry Perry skates up to us and plays *Red House* by Jimi Hendrix. He has an electric guitar and microphone hooked up to a little amplifier in a satchel draped over his shoulder. He's on roller skates and has a big, white turban.

Harry Perry is a Venice Beach institution, an icon on the boardwalk, everybody knows him. He came to Venice in 1974. In the early 1990s, LA County attempted to gentrify Venice Beach. Ordinances were passed against street performances: "No person shall hawk, peddle or vend any goods, wares or merchandise, or beg or solicit alms or donations upon" any sidewalk, boardwalk, or public way adjoining a specified length of the Pacific Ocean, including the area known as the Venice Beach Boardwalk. So, Harry Perry led a group of 27 Venice Beach performers in a class-action lawsuit against the Los Angeles Police Department and the ordinances. After many years of litigation, the court ruled in favor of Harry Perry and his co-plaintiffs. The Los Angeles City Council then created new legislation that severely restricted performance rather than banning it altogether. Harry Perry alleged that the combination of gentrification and restrictions threatened to destroy the atmosphere that made Venice Beach the social mecca.

After Harry Perry finishes playing his song, I ask him a question, and he doesn't answer. I give him a couple of dollars, and away he skates.

I ask Bruce, "Why does he wear that turban?"

"I heard he's a Sikh."

Sikhism is the world's fifth-largest religion. The core pillars are sharing with others, helping those in need, and participating as part of a community. A spirit of giving, sharing, and caring for one another is central to Sikhism; also, earning a living honestly without exploitation or fraud, speaking the truth at all times, and meditating on God's name to live a life of decency and humility.

As we continue to talk, I say, "Hey, I got fired by the Chinese restaurant, so I don't have anything to do in the day anymore. I was thinking of putting out a blanket and writing poetry. I could tell people, 'Name me any subject in the world, and I will write you a poem about it.' What do you think? Do you think that would work?"

Bruce says, "Sure, all these other fuckers are doing it. Why can't you?"

That day, I decided to be a poet on Venice Beach.

Name Me Any Subject In The World

A few days pass and I get up enough nerve to write poetry on the Venice Beach Boardwalk. It is Saturday. I park my car as usual in the Rose Avenue parking lot and pull out a wooden wine box from my trunk. I walk down the boardwalk to the end of Dudley Avenue, right down from the Cadillac Hotel, built in 1914 and once it is said was a summer residence for Charlie Chaplin. I open the wine box containing an old Mexican blanket I bought years before and some plastic-sleeved pages of my writing. I lay down the blanket on the edge of the boardwalk and put out a few pages of my writing. I place the empty wine box out for tips and use the cover as a sign that reads POETRY FOR PEACE. I sit for a full hour before anyone comes up to me. My first customer asks for some obscure subject, probably just to throw me off, and I write them a poem about it. They say, "Wow, that's pretty good," and drop a dollar in the wine box. *I guess that first day I made about five or ten dollars. I was elated. I was an artist, a real poet that could write improvisational poetry. What fulfillment I felt. I was now a busker.*

The crowds get bigger. Some days, I have ten to fifteen people waiting to get a poem, all standing around and watching me write. Some of the homeless people begin to take notice as well. They gather and watch. There is Big Mary. She is a heavy-set Black lady from the South, maybe Alabama or Mississippi. She doesn't take no shit from anybody. She will throw down with the toughest man. A real badass. A woman who can be your worst enemy or best friend. Mary has a heart of gold and is concerned about the other homeless people, a kind of mother to the beach. There is Vino, a street savvy lighter-skinned Black dude who is always working some sort of angle, trying to make some deal to get paid. It seems to me he is a bit twitchy. The kind of guy that will do almost anything to survive, and everyone knows it. He has only one way to live: for himself. *Over one summer, I saw him become a full-fledged crackhead; yet he was still my friend.* There is Crazy Mary, this crazy-ass White girl, skinny as a rail, always screaming incoherently about something. No one ever understands a damn thing she says; we all just steer clear of her. I try to at least be nice. Soon, she says she is in love with me. If at all possible, I avoid being alone with her. *One night, I tried to talk to her alone, and she ended up swiping my 12-pack; she was wild.* There is David, a Black kid that is too young to be homeless. He is very bright and has the best attitude of any one on the beach. He must have come from a good home because he has some real nice stuff. Kind of a hippie, he's always talking about religion and philosophy. *I liked him the minute I met him. We had some great talks. I always thought it was too bad he was down here with us.*

These are just a few of the homeless people who stay down by Dudley Avenue; there are many more, a true cast of characters. Almost all of them Black people, and I am the only White guy. Oh, there is one other older White guy, James; he keeps to himself, never talks much to me or anyone else. You always see him riding his bike alone.

This was how it started. I remember many days of writing poetry on the boardwalk. I continued to draw pride in myself for being able to be a real artist, free from any past, just in the moment.

Some evenings, after writing in the day, I head to Michael's restaurant to work. I am doing great at the job. They must be impressed with my work, the manager is about to make me a waiter, which will mean a lot more money. It is all working out. I even pick up some day shifts. Even so, I am still sleeping in my car.

***

Today, I am walking on the boardwalk and go into this tattoo shop. I have been wanting another tattoo and have decided to get a Yin and Yang on my right shoulder. I only have one tattoo from years before, a little one of Aces and Eights on my left shoulder called the Dead Man's Hand. *Ironically, I remember the night I got it back in Denver, I got jumped by about eight guys. They beat me within an inch of my life. I never did like this tattoo after that. I eventually got it covered over with another tattoo taken from a cylinder seal from the third millennium B.C., depicting the solar system as it was known to the Sumerians. The system consists of twelve celestial bodies; The twelfth planet, known as Nibiru, is on an elongated, 3,600-year-long, elliptical orbit around the Sun.*

***

One day, after working the lunch shift at Michael's, I drive to Venice to see what's going on. I see Bruce right off, and he asks, "Mike, you think you can drive me up to Pico and Vermont? I need to pick up some weed."

"Right now? Do you have any money for gas?"

He does, so we head over to my car and along the way, two other Black guys walk up to us. One is kind of short and knows Bruce well. He gives him a handshake and hug.

Bruce says, "Mike, this is Quentin; he's a good friend of mine."

"How are you doing, Quentin?"

"Good to meet you, Mike."

The other guy is tall and slim. Not skinny, just slim. He is a little darker than Bruce and is quiet and suspiciously looking around.

Bruce introduces me to him, "Mike, this is Roland."

"Hey, what's up?" I say.

He doesn't say a thing, just looks at me, a look of fuck off. I think, what the fuck is this guy's problem. I have to watch out for him.

So, all four of us hop in my car and head to the corner of West Pico Boulevard and Vermont Avenue. I am driving, Bruce is in the front passenger's seat, Roland is sitting behind him, and Quentin is sitting behind me. Almost immediately after we get in the car, an argument breaks out. All three of them are speaking, or should I say shouting, at the same time. Then, it is just Bruce and Roland arguing.

Bruce says to Roland, "Motherfucker, you don't know jack-shit about what you're saying. You are one dumbass country motherfucker that don't know shit about nothing."

Roland leans up in the seat and points his finger at Bruce. "Motherfucker, I will beat your motherfucking ass. You don't know who the fuck you're talking to. Don't make me fuck you up, right here. Just keep pushing me, motherfucker, I'm gonna show you."

Back and forth it goes. I'm afraid they are going to start punching each other right there, inside my car.

After about ten minutes of this shit, I ask them, "Hey, can you guys please stop arguing for just a minute? I am getting a fucking headache."

I remember thinking to myself, damn, do Black people always fucking argue? I had not been around very many Black people up to that point in my life, I was still a bit naive. Although, I had been around a lot of arguing, that's for sure. I thought, damn where does all this anger come from?

After I tell them to stop arguing, Roland offhandedly tells Bruce, "And this fucking peckerwood driving ain't got no right to be talking to me about shit anyway. I don't even know who this motherfucker is. For all I know, he might even be a fucking cop."

I wasn't too streetwise at that point, although I did know if someone said you were a cop, you couldn't let that go.

I turn my head around and tell him straight to his face, "My name is not fucking peckerwood; my name is Mike, understand? You are going to get that straight, or I am going to pull the fucking car over, and all of you can get the fuck out. And I ain't no fucking cop."

Roland looks at me with disgust and continues to argue with Bruce. It's awful. You can cut the tension with a knife. Soon, he nonchalantly refers to me as peckerwood, again. I slam on the brakes, squealing the tires, and pull over to the side of Venice Boulevard. "Get out."

All three of them look at me, stunned, thinking, "What? Who the fuck is this White-boy? He can't tell us shit."

I say again louder, "Get the fuck out."

There is a long pause of uncomfortable silence. Roland is looking at me with a kind of puzzled look on his face then he breaks into the biggest smile. "Come on, Mike. Take it fucking easy; you ain't got to get so mad about some dumb shit. Damn, you's a bad motherfucker, Mike. This White-boy's got heart, Bruce. Where the fuck did you find this motherfucker? Come on, Mike, I won't call you that no more. Let's go man. It's cool."

I turn around one more time and say, "Okay, so what's my name?" *When I asked this, though they didn't know it, I felt like bursting into tears. I was so nervous.*

"Mike, Mike."

We all start laughing, and I take off again.

From that day, Roland was my constant friend and brother; for some reason, he never saw me as White, or the White he hated. I guess he saw me as just a man with no color. I also remember on that day in the car how relieved I was after he smiled. Roland could have killed me.

A little later, on this same drive, I tell them, "Do you guys have to keep saying the N-word? Can you please not say it around me?"

Bruce says, "What the fuck do you know about that Mike? I can say whatever the fuck I want."

"Yes, I know that. It's just that the N-word is a stupid word. Why use a name that racist White people called Black people and call each other the same name? That don't make no sense to me."

"You don't know shit, Mike," Bruce says.

"Well, I hope I don't start calling myself Honky or

Cracker."

They all laugh.

Later on the ride, I have to tell them again, "Can you please not say the N-word around me, not even to each other?"

We talk for about a minute more on the subject, and someone says, "Can you try to just drive the fucking car safe and shut the fuck up."

"Okay, if you do, motherfucker," I say.

As long as Bruce and Roland were my friends, every time they used the N-word, I would say, don't say it around me. I tell people today not to ever say that word around me. A word once used for ridicule cannot be turned into praise. I will not participate in any form of racist behavior; I strive in my life not to ever be ignorant about anything.

***

Roland has been in and out of prison all his life. In California, I think he says he did a five year stint at the Chuckawalla Valley State Prison and another four years at Ironwood State Prison. Before that, I am not sure where he did his time.

He once tells me, "Mike, in prison, they used to call me the Devil. All those motherfuckers in there were scared of me. They all thought I was an evil, ruthless motherfucker. Even the guards didn't mess with me. They all knew I would fuck them up." He was so proud of that. He might have told me he killed some people before. He said he was from Illinois, or maybe it was the South.

Roland is a direct product of the racist American system. A Black man who has been told since birth that he is nothing. A Black man who was fucked over, in some way, by every White person he ever dealt with. After a while, this man or any man, will turn to rage. Roland has turned to rage. Poverty is the worst form of violence; it perpetuates it. Now, I am not saying Roland is a good man to people. To me he is my brother; to other people, especially to White people, he is their worst nightmare. He is a very scary guy.

***

It is a beautiful Sunday in the spring of 1991; the crowds at Venice Beach have been growing with the start of the season. People are everywhere, and I am busy writing poetry. Over a period of three hours, I have already written twenty poems or more, from subjects such as love, to something as far out as a dinosaur. It takes real craft to be an improvisational poet. The people love it, I have about $10 in the tip box and $40 in my pocket. As a busker, you never leave too much of your tips out for people to see.

Sitting around with me are Bruce, Big Mary, and this other big Black kid I don't know. This kid is about six foot two or three, maybe, around 250 pounds. Huge. He's about 21. He doesn't speak, just sits there watching.

Bruce finally introduces him to me. "Mike, this is Big Homie."

I say, "What's up?"

He just looks at me with a blank face. For a second, I think maybe he can't speak, maybe he has a disability.

Then, I realize he is choosing to just ignore me. *Big Homie did not trust any White people. Well, he didn't trust any people, and he especially did not like White people, so he wouldn't even acknowledge I existed. He struck me as a big, goofy kid, and I wasn't going to try and convince a youngster to be respectful.*

Eventually, up walks Roland. He says right off, "Mike, you don't know jack-motherfucking-shit about no motherfucking poetry. What the fuck is this shit?"

"Name me any subject in the world, and I will write you a poem about it," I tell him.

"My ass. This is some fucking White-boy bullshit, Mike; you know that."

From behind me, Big Mary tells Roland, "Shut the fuck up and sit the fuck down."

He turns toward her, "Bitch, don't you tell me a motherfucking thing, unless you want to get knocked the fuck out."

She jumps to her feet, throws her arms out wide, and says, "Bring it on, motherfucker. Let's go."

They argue until finally Roland sits down, watches the people come up to me, and is quiet, thank goodness. It is rumored that Big Mary always carries a knife; she is the only person on the beach that Roland will not fuck with.

So, they all just hang around and participate in the atmosphere, kind of like TV for the homeless.

At a lull in the day, I turn to Bruce and Roland, "You know what I really need is a couple of guys to go into the crowd and bring the customers. That way we could make more money, and you guys would have something to do, other than sitting on your asses around here and fucking up my program, always arguing. What do you say, will you do it?"

Roland says, "I ain't doing that shit. You want them, you go get them yourself."

Bruce gets up. "Okay, I will do it. I can do that." He disappears into the crowd, going up to everyone he sees and asks, "Do you like poetry? Name me any subject in the world, and I'll write you a poem about it."

The people say, "No way, how are you going to do that?"

He says, "I guarantee it. I'll write you a poem about any subject. How about it? You want to do it? Follow me."

Once any of them say yes, he brings them over to me, I write them a poem, and he goes into the crowd again. The money starts rolling in. At the end of that first day, I split $80 in tips with Bruce, and now we have a little partnership. After a couple of days, Roland is out in the crowd too. He isn't as good as Bruce, probably just too mean-looking, but he starts bringing a few customers. I sit there with my hair hanging down over my face and write, almost non-stop. I need more pens and paper. That day, we make $130, which I split evenly between myself, Bruce, and Roland. After a while, I even cut Big Homie in for a share of the money.

"You're security," I tell him. He agrees.

That became the little homeless crew that I started to roll with: Bruce, Roland, me, and Big Homie. Although it took Big Homie about a month before he ever spoke to me. He would walk about six feet behind us, kind of like a curious admirer. He was big enough to have been a middle linebacker in the NFL, probably just never got a chance to play any ball. It was good to have him around, though. With time, we became close friends. This was our little gang, three hardcore Black guys and a White guy from Colorado. No one would fuck around with any of us; they knew they would get fucked up if they had to deal with Roland or Big Homie, and no one wanted that.

At night, I still drive somewhere away from everyone to sleep alone in my car. It is my quiet time from the fast-paced restaurant or the crazy homeless life of Venice Beach. I enjoy both very much; sometimes though, after writing or running food all day, I am drained. I tell myself, I am not at the bottom, I have my car, my art and my job, so all is possible.

***

Some days, for a little mental relaxation, I ride my bike over to the Venice canals and go across the cool bridges or ride on the walkways. It is like a little haven there. *Before I became homeless, when I was staying at an international hostel called Nice Place in Santa Monica at 1235 10th Street, I got a nice bike, a Specialized Rockhopper. I keep it in my trunk. People say it is a $1,000 bike; I got it used.* Six blocks of the original canals still remain; they're just south of Venice Boulevard and west of Ocean Avenue, one reaches all the way to Marina Del Rey. There are four east-west canals (Carroll Canal, Linnie Canal, Howland Canal, and Sherman Canal) and two north-south canals (Eastern Canal and Grand Canal). The canals were renovated in 1992 and reopened in 1993. The water enters through sea gates in the Marina Del Rey breakwater, and again in Washington Boulevard.

On the way back from the canals, I ride by the traffic

circle at Windward Avenue and Main Street which is located on top of what was once the Venice Lagoon. At Windward Avenue and Pacific Avenue is the VENICE sign which spans across Windward Avenue; it is a modern-day replica of the one installed in 1905. Venice is home to a large number of early 1900s buildings that emulate Italian Renaissance architecture, particularly along Windward Avenue. In 1957, the Orson Wells movie *Touch of Evil*, converted this part of Venice into a Mexican border town and installed a border crossing on Ocean Front Walk.

Occasionally, I go to lunch around the corner at The Sidewalk Cafe, at 1401 Ocean Front Walk, by the end of Horizon Avenue. I get a burger and a beer, and sit on the patio, girl watching. I always go next door to Small World Books and sit and read from some of the most interesting books. I usually end up buying one, if I have enough money. Then I ride back by The Potter, at 1305 Ocean Front Walk. It's a four-story building built in 1912 and the oldest remaining beach-front hotel in Los Angeles, called Venice Beach Suites & Hotel. Then I pass by the Blu House at 523 Ocean Front Walk, built in 1901, and the Gingerbread Court building at 517 Ocean Front Park, built in 1922.

***

Tonight, Bruce, Roland, and I are heading back to Pico and Vermont. I'm driving them again. Big Homie almost doesn't come; he doesn't trust a White man to drive him around. Especially one he still thinks is a cop. Damn, I'm homeless too. It takes him three months before he believes I am not a cop. I'm not quite sure Big Homie is too bright. He has a kind heart though, after you get by all the indoctrinated bullshit armor. So, on the drive, all four of us finally have a chance to talk it over. I purposely ask them, "So, what do you think about White people?"

Roland says, "I hate fucking White people, every motherfucking White person I ever dealt with fucked me over."

Big Homie chimes in, "I hate White people, too. I don't trust any of them."

Bruce kind of agrees, "White people have fucked me over too. I don't really hate them all, I just don't want anything to do with most of them."

"What about me? I'm White," I say.

Roland and Bruce both say, "Ah, Mike, you're different. You ain't White. You're Black."

After a couple of minutes, I see Roland smiling through the rear view mirror, and he jokingly says, "You still got a whole lot to learn, though, Mike, about being Black. I'll try to fucking school you, even though it might not fucking help. We'll still try to show you how to be Black."

Bruce says, "Yeah, that's right, Mike. We're going to show you how to be Black. Just stick with me, Mike, I'll show you how to get paid."

Roland immediately says to Bruce, "Motherfucker, you're sleeping on the fucking ground."

Bruce replies, "Yeah, alright, well. I always got money in my pocket, fucker, and you ain't got shit."

That is how they felt about me, that I'm not White. I am not quite sure why. Maybe it's because I see them not as

Black either; they are just my friends.

I begin to confide more and more with Roland. He becomes my street mentor. Bruce is too loud and obnoxious. He thinks he is smarter than everyone else and has a way of making a person feel worse when he gives advice. All I want is to have a friend to bullshit with, not another dad to tell me how bad of a fuck-up I am. So, I slowly begin to see Bruce more and more as a kind of foe. Not because he is a bad person—well, he is a little bit, just not completely. Also, Big Homie is just a big kid; he is like a dog that has been kicked too much, so he isn't a friend I can confide in either. It doesn't help that it takes him a long time to trust me.

So, my friendship and brotherhood with Roland begin to grow. We walk around the boardwalk and talk it over. He is a real smart guy, after you get past all the anger and pain. He is raw and always tells the straight truth, as he sees it. This is a real interest of mine, to try and understand the world of a strong, Black man. Roland is my trusted guide and protector. I owe him for showing me how not to be even a little racist, you know, that kind of racism you don't know you have, that you have just accepted from your youth, and how you were brought up. He actually shows me how to find peace, kind of strange, seeing that he is a man of war. He has seen many terrible things and really just wants to be normal. Deep down, I don't think he wants to hurt others; it is his defensive mechanism.

I guess for Roland I am a brother that will never fuck him over, and he really appreciates that. I see him as a wise man, not a homeless, broke motherfucker. The mistake most people make is to see him as a harmless piece of shit, that is right before they get grabbed by the shirt or hit in the head with a bottle. That is the root of his rage, the need to be seen as a strong man. It makes me feel uncomfortable when Roland accosts someone. That is not my way. I will not hit another person unless I am hit first, at least that's what I tell myself. Roland will just walk up and punch someone.

Today, Roland and I are walking on the boardwalk. He is bumping into everyone. He tells me, "I don't break my stride for anyone; if they are in my way, I walk straight the fuck through them. Fuck all these motherfuckers." This approach might work on any small town sidewalk, but not on the Venice Beach Boardwalk where there are thousands of people. As he bumps into them, if someone takes offense, he jumps in their face and says, "What's your problem, motherfucker? Can't you see I'm walking here? Get the fuck out of my way."

If they reply with anything other than an apology, he pushes them. He has no fear. Most people flee at that point, but for those that don't, Roland smacks them on the side of the head.

I think, hey, these people are just trying to have a good time in Venice, they don't want to go to the hospital. After this conflict happens many times, I ask Roland, "Why do you keep messing with people?"

He says, "Mike, fuck these people. They got no right to be on my boardwalk."

"Your boardwalk? This is not your boardwalk."

"It is now."

I guess that is how he lives his life; wherever he is, he

thinks all of it is his. Part of my impression is, wow, this is kind-of exciting, and another part is a mild disgust. That's how it is being homeless; you have to find the best in all situations. At least Roland is my friend, and he protects me.

***

Today, I am riding my bike on the boardwalk; I stop for a quick rest, and this guy comes up to me. He has his dog on a leash. I have seen him around. He is respected on the beach; most people speak highly of him, a standup guy. He knows me.

He says, "What's up, Mike?"

"Nothing much, just enjoying the day."

"Hey, do you mind if I borrow your bike for a minute? I only have to go a couple of blocks away, I just don't want to have to walk over there. I promise, I'll be right back. It'll be real quick. Five minutes max."

I say, "No."

"Okay, what if I leave my dog, Wolf, with you. That way you'll know I ain't trying to fuck you over."

"Okay, I guess. How long are you going to be?"

"Only about five minutes. Real quick. I'll be right back."

"Okay, then. Come back."

He takes off on my bike and never returns. Now I have a dog and no bike.

Wolf was a great animal, a real beautiful soul. I was not a big fan of German Shepherds, and continue not to be, but Wolf was different. He was so smart and gentle. Although, this was another mouth I had to put food in. Damn, all I wanted was to be self-sufficient; the world wanted more than that from me.

Soon after, I tell Bruce and Roland about my bike being stolen. Roland immediately goes out on the prowl to find the guy who stole it and fuck him up. Bruce has another point of view; he likes dogs and instantly thinks Wolf is his. Now I'm out of a bike and a dog. Around the same time, the starter goes out on my car; it's stranded in the Rose parking lot. So, I don't have a running car or my bike to get to work, and one day, I just decide not to show up. That is the end of my job at Michael's restaurant. *I guess I thought it was too much to be homeless and try to be normal, so I quit.*

The last night before quitting, I come back to my car after a long shift at Michael's, exhausted, and Wolf is sleeping in my back seat, where I sleep. Bruce is there, and other people are sitting in my car that I don't know.

Earlier that day, Bruce asks, "Mike, you're gonna be at work all day anyway, so can I borrow the keys? I just want to stay cool and sit in the car while you're gone? Come on, man, help me out."

"Okay, just don't fuck it up, though. I only want you in the car, no one else, please. Can you do that for me?"

"Sure, Mike. No problem."

That night, as I get back from work, I say, "What the fuck is Wolf doing sleeping where I sleep?"

Bruce says, "Come on, man, he's just taking a little nap."

"Get him the fuck out of there. And who are these other fuckers in my car? Everybody has got to get out now."

That is the way with Bruce; there is always something about him that just doesn't give a shit about anybody else. Sooner or later, everything Bruce touches is going to get fucked up. My compromise is to quit my job and keep the fucking dog and other people out of my sleeping quarters. I am not afraid of Bruce. *After a time being homeless, you just don't give a shit. There are things much worse than fighting. In this life you have to stand up for yourself, and if anyone, especially Bruce, doesn't agree, fuck him.*

After that, the little .22 caliber pistol I keep in the trunk, which was given to me by my grandfather, magically disappears. I ask Bruce about it.

Of course he says, "I didn't see no pistol, Mike. I didn't see anything like that." Which is a fucking lie; he took it.

So, eventually, I take all my belongings out of the trunk and hide them behind a synagogue called The Pacific Jewish Center, also known as The Shul on the Beach at 505 Ocean Front Walk. *I was always appreciative that no one ever took my stuff or messed with it. Included in my stuff were a double-breasted black suit, a couple of silk shirts, a pair of Italian black shoes and black socks, and my writing packed into two wine boxes. I could never believe that I kept all my writing throughout this whole time of being homeless.*

***

About a month after my bike is stolen, I am standing on the boardwalk alone, and here walks up the guy that stole it. He is with a stone-cold Crip. After living in the hood for a while, you get to know the real gangsters, and this guy was straight OG. I think, definitely a killer. They walk straight up to me—well the Crip kind of dances while he walks, kind of like running and walking. For all those that haven't lived in the hood, it is known as the Crip walk. You notice it real quick.

The guy who stole my bike asks, "Where is my dog?"

"Where is my bike?"

The Crip quickly jumps up in my face, "Motherfucker, we didn't ask you about no motherfucking bike; you understand. You answer his questions, or I'm gonna fuck you up right here."

I usually am not afraid of anyone, although I can honestly say I was afraid of this Crip. I say, "Okay."

The thief asks again, "So where is my dog, motherfucker?"

My car has become a safe haven for people to take naps. Most nights, I now sleep on the ground. This night, Roland is in the front seat sleeping, and despite all my efforts, Wolf is in the back seat. So, I have this fucking killer in my face, and I get this epiphany. I say, "Oh, Wolf is in my car right over there."

The Crip says, "That one right there, that's your fucking car?"

I point to it. "Yeah, that's the one." They both turn and start to walk toward it. At about the fourth step, I say to them, "Hey, when you're getting him, just make sure you don't wake up Roland. He's sleeping in the front seat."

They both stop dead in their tracks, even the Crip; it is amazing to see. Roland's reputation has filtered throughout the beach; no one, not even killers, want to fuck with him. I guess everyone knows Roland has only two ways to go—

death or victory. He is not to be messed with. They both turn around and walk back to me.

The Crip jumps in my face again, this time so close I can feel his breath. He says, "Motherfucker, if you don't bring his fucking dog back, I'm going to come back down here, and you don't want that. If I gotta come back down here, I'll kill your motherfucking ass. You understand, punk?"

"No problem, man. I'll take care of it. I got it."

They leave. *I never took the dog back, and they never came back. Besides, how was I supposed to return Wolf when his former owner was homeless. So, fuck him and that Crip. Also, wow, it was good to have a killer like Roland as a friend in the hood.*

***

It is a beautiful summer in 1991 in Venice. Why do I need a job waiting tables? Heck I can make all the money I need just by writing poetry. I have my car as a place of refuge, so fuck it, I am an artist. *I had left all the niceties of the civilized world. I was living on a day-to-day basis. I remember being hungry some days and not always being okay; it was just that California was the place for me. I was living free here.*

***

Today, Bruce and I are walking on the boardwalk with Wolf on his chain beside Bruce. Out of nowhere this fucking vicious pitbull comes charging up to Wolf, and they start fighting. I am trying to break it up when I see that the pitbull is about to bite Wolf on the jugular. I kick the pitbull in the ribs as hard as I can, sending his ass flying. I like Wolf, no other dog is going to mess him up when I'm around. The pitbull runs away, whimpering. Wolf has some deep scratches and bite marks, he's messed up. We take him back to my car and put him in the back seat. As soon as we get him in there, the fucking pitbull comes running back. He's intimidating. We are sitting in my car with the windows rolled up and the pitbull is trying his best to break in. He finally leaves, thank goodness.

Afterward, Bruce and I go to this little store to get Wolf some hydrogen peroxide and ointment for his wounds. The Korean shopkeepers follow us around the entire time. I tell them, "Damn, can't I even shop without you staring at me; I'm not taking anything."

"You hurry up and buy," they tell us.

We get what we need and fix Wolf up the best we can. He is feeling kind of rough, and I let him stay in my back seat for a few days. I come back one evening from being somewhere, and Bruce tells me, "Wolf is really bad, he won't get out of the car to eat or drink. He's really out of it, I think he's going to die."

So, I check on him and quietly whisper in his ear, "Wolf if you don't get up now, you're gonna die. You have to get up and drink water and eat some food, that is the only way you are going to get better. Now, come on, get up and eat. Come on, let's go."

Wolf slowly rises up and magically, as if it is a miracle, hops out and eats and drinks. *I was so happy, I loved Wolf.*

***

Tonight, Bruce, Roland, and I walk down to the Santa Monica Pier for a free concert with The Bonedaddys, a worldbeat party band. We didn't know who was playing, we found out when we got there. We have three bottles of Cisco and are getting drunk. If you have lived in the hood, you know about Cisco; we call it crack in a bottle. That shit will make you lose your mind.

As we walk, Bruce goes up to everyone he sees and says, "Do you have a little something for the homeless. I wouldn't ask, it's just that I don't have anywhere to sleep tonight, you know? I'm on the ground. Anything you have to give would really be a big help. Anything; penny, nickel, dime." Then he smiles and just looks at them. People eventually come out of their pockets with a few dollars. As we walk away, Bruce tells me, "See, Mike, that's how you get paid. You got to spread your hustle."

I say, kind of joking, "Man, have some respect for yourself; don't be asking people for money, at least not around me. And you know what you need to do is get a fucking job, and get up off your broke ass, and stop bullshitting."

"I don't need no motherfucking job, Mike. I'm the King of Miami, and you don't know shit. I'm gonna be me, and that's it."

"Man, all I am saying is you can't be fucking begging. There is a certain minimum standard as a healthy young man; you got to support yourself."

Roland jumps in, "That's right, motherfucker; don't be

fucking begging no one around me."

"Fuck that." Bruce always likes to stretch out the T sound on the end of the word, that. "I'm getting paid, so fuck all y'all."

Bruce is almost never hungry, and most of the time, he has money in his pocket. It isn't really begging to him, it is more about getting paid. The real fact is he just wants to talk to everyone he sees. He figures by walking up to them and asking for some money, he will get to talk to them. Then, he can ramble on and on about his life story to a complete stranger. It isn't that he wants to be their friend; it is that he is a little bit too civil to just take their money and walk away. Basically, he wants to control everybody he sees, and get paid to do it.

Roland and I walk a long ways away, and Roland shouts back to him, "Come on, Bruce, move your fucking ass. We ain't waiting for you."

Bruce hollers back, "I'll be right there. I'll catch up."

He eventually does. Bruce just loves to talk.

Along the way to the Pier, there is an open park, Crescent Bay Park. There are some homeless people in sleeping bags spread out across the park. Roland sees this as a great opportunity—time to get paid. He is almost gleeful. He picks up an empty bottle and has it in his hand as he walks up to everyone he sees from then on, looking at them, sizing them up. Finally, there is this one White guy sleeping in an almost brand new sleeping bag. His gear looks like he has money and that maybe he is sleeping in the park for just one night. Roland walks to him and hoists him straight up in his bag. He tells the waking guy, "What was once yours is now mine." He hits the guy over the head with the bottle. Down the guy goes, knocked out. Roland goes through his pockets, takes everything he's got.

As we leave, I look down at the guy, and he has blood on his head. I think, my goodness, why am I hanging out with this vicious psychopath motherfucker, Roland. I tell him, "Can you please stop your fucking bullshit? I can't be hanging around you motherfucker if you are going to get me jammed up. Can you try and not put us all in fucking jail? Is that too motherfucking much to ask? Please."

"Come on, Mike. That motherfucker don't mean nothing; it's just money."

"Can you please not do that shit around me?"

He says in laughter, "You afraid to go to jail, Mike? Is that what it is, you're afraid of big, bad jail? I bet that's it. You ain't never been to jail, have you Mike? Hear that Bruce? Mike is scared of a little jail."

"No, I'm not afraid of fucking jail. I just don't want to see you kill somebody in front of me, if you don't fucking mind."

We then pass by the old shuttered Club Casa del Mar, a private beach club that opened on May 1, 1926, designed to reflect an Italian Renaissance Revival aesthetic. The hotel's glory days spanned from 1926 to 1941, as it became one of the most successful beach clubs in Southern California, popular with socialites and Hollywood celebrities; there are 129 rooms, a curving double staircase, a high-coffered ceiling, mosaic tile floors, and glowing copper sconces atop mahogany pillars in the lobby. The ballroom, with floor-to-ceiling windows facing the ocean, seats up to 270 guests.

Later that night, after the concert, we are walking on a bike path between some houses, and two cops on bikes stop us. "What are you doing?" they ask.

I am drunk and tell them, "Damn, isn't there any crime in Compton? Why are you jacking us? We didn't do nothing. Can't I even walk in my own neighborhood, without getting harassed? I thought we still lived in the United States of America. Don't we have rights as American citizens?" Bruce and Roland try to get me to shut up, and I keep telling the cops to leave us alone.

Finally, the cops go, and Bruce and Roland tell me, "If you were Black, you would've went to jail."

I remember thinking to myself, so the only reason I wasn't in jail was because I was White? Good, then I might have kept us all out of jail. It kind of made me proud.

***

Today, we all go to one of the beach restrooms to clean up. Shaving, brushing our teeth, all the regular stuff. We use the showers outside, you know, the ones for the surfers; sometimes we just take the shower with our clothes on. You get to shower and do your laundry at the same time. Bruce and Roland are done first, and me and Big Homie are finishing up in the restroom. Big Homie steps outside to have a smoke. As I am taking a leak, this guy comes out of nowhere and stands beside me. He looks at me and says, "I'll suck your dick, if you want me to."

I look at him and say, "Get the fuck out of here. Can't I even take a fucking piss without some motherfucker asking to suck my dick? Get the fuck away from me."

The guy quickly walks out of the restroom.

Big Homie comes back in after a minute and sees that I am pissed. He asks, "What's up?"

"This fucking guy just asked to suck my dick, right here when I was taking a piss. What the fuck?"

"Who is it?"

We walk out of the restroom, and the guy is about 40 yards away. I point him out. Big Homie immediately goes after him; the guy has his back to us, so he doesn't see him coming. I see Big Homie walk up to him, say something, then bam, with one punch, knocks him out. The guy drops on the sand next to the bike path, and Big Homie nonchalantly walks back to the restroom to get his toothpaste and shaving gel. *It stuck in my memory that we walked right past the guy laid out next to the path. I felt so sorry for him.*

***

One day, I am walking with Roland on the boardwalk. I tell him, "I wish I was Black."

He looks over at me and says, "Mike, you ain't Black. You're White, and that's all you're ever gonna to be."

He means it with the highest respect. I think he sees it as a wonderful thing for a White guy to say. I meant it, too. *There is something really special about Black people. Hearing all the stories of how these friends of mine have been abused by the American system, opened my mind. I was brought up with all White people, and I had seen some of the sins of their character. I do not want any part of the hypocrisy anymore. I am changing, never to return to the man I used to be.*

***

This morning, Roland, Bruce, and I are sitting in my car thinking about what we should do for some fun today. I tell them, "Hey, maybe we should go play some basketball." They finally agree. So, we walk down to the courts right next to Muscle Beach. You might have heard of Muscle Beach in Venice, that is where Schwarzenegger used to work out sometimes. I think Ferrigno did, too. These basketball courts are the same that they play on in *White Men Can't Jump*. On one of the courts there are three White guys playing, and we ask if they would like a game, three on three. They agree. As the game starts, Bruce and Roland give me shit that I don't know how to play. It's true, I ain't too good at dribbling, and I can't jump that high, but I can shoot. *That day, I made them eat their words, I hit shot after shot. They were so happy. We won three games in a row.*

***

Today, it is a beautiful sunny day, and I am busy writing poetry. My brain is hurting from all the pressure of writing about every subject in the world. It isn't easy to do; I love it though. The regular homeless crowd has gathered around, and as usual, Roland is pissed at the world. Blah, blah, blah, he goes on and on about everything—how the world is all fucked up and everyone in it is fucked up. Then, he decides to pick on me.

Roland announces to everyone around, "Look at Mike; he don't belong around here. We all know that, Mike. What gives you the right to sit here and write poetry? You are just a rich White man trying to act poor. You ought to go on back home, and you know it. You don't know nothing about slumming like the rest of us. You had it easy growing up."

I point my finger at him and say, "Hey, man, I don't want to hear your motherfucking bullshit, you understand? Don't fucking talk about me. You don't know jack-shit about me, so don't say a fucking thing. Got it, motherfucker?"

"Yeah, right, I know about you. You are just the same as all the rest of them, the same as all the rest of the motherfucking White people I knew all my life."

I jump up from my writing, run over, and kick a garbage barrel next to him; it goes flying. It is not too smart either because I am barefooted and almost break my foot. It's worth it, though. Then I turn and walk out onto the beach. I think, why is the world so mean? Why don't people just love one another? Does it always have to be about race? Do people always have to argue? Why? Tears begin to flow down my face. I walk about 100 feet on the sand, sit down, and just cry for a minute. I have my back to the boardwalk to make sure no one sees my tears.

Later, people told me that back on the boardwalk, Big Mary and Bruce started giving Roland shit.

Big Mary says, "Roland, you better go tell that good man you're sorry. You are one dumb motherfucker. He has been really nice to you, and you don't even give a shit. You're just a broke down, bitter motherfucker. You better get off your ass and go out there."

Bruce joins in, "Fuck that, Roland. You ain't gonna fuck up my money. We got a good thing going here with this little poetry thing. You ain't going to fuck it up for me. Go and tell him you're sorry. Do it motherfucker."

Finally, Roland walks out to me on the sand. As he approaches, I am wiping the last tears from my eyes. When Roland looks at my face, he has the most overwhelming look of compassion. It is almost like he just wants to hug me and tell me it's okay. Roland doesn't hug anybody.

He says, "Come on, Mike, I'm sorry. I don't know why I said that shit. You know me, Mike, I'm an angry fucker; you know that. Come on, man, you know you're my brother, Mike. Let's just forget about what I was saying and just be cool, again. Okay?"

"I am not like every other White person. I am not mean, and I don't want to hurt anyone. All I want is for everyone to be at peace, you know that."

"I know, Mike. Let's go back to the boardwalk. Come on, man, let's go back to the boardwalk."

I soon say okay.

***

This morning, I go out on to the Venice Breakwater directly off the end of Windward Avenue. It is a huge rock wall which Abbot Kinney built in 1905; 60 feet long and about 20 feet tall. I want to walk out there and see the ocean better. When I reach the north end of the wall, I sit there, relaxing. I see this huge wave mounting up in front of me. I think, is that wave going to hit me? I hold on to the rock for dear life, and boom, I get blasted. I try to get across the rocks as fast as I can; only now they are all wet, and I am slipping. Boom, the second wave hits me. Now I have to cling to the rock to keep from being washed out to sea. I have to get out of here now, or I might be killed. Boom, the third wave hits me. Still, I hold on to the rocks, thank goodness, and I make it back to dry land.

***

On this night, Bruce and I are walking on the boardwalk to go get a slice of pizza at Gabriella's New York City Pizza stand by Westminster Avenue. They are the only thing that stays open late. The boardwalk is usually pretty empty at night. As we get close to the place, there is this one Mexican guy standing on the side of the boardwalk. We walk by, and he cusses us in Spanish.

By this time, I know a little Spanish, and I reply, "Cállate la boca." *Shut the fuck up.*

He just smiles at me and cusses me more.

I tell him, "Patearé tu maldito trasero." *I will kick your fucking ass.*

He pulls out a knife. For some reason, it doesn't scare me. I go to push him. He slices me across the hand, and my blood starts flowing. I am so fucking pissed, I start to charge him. Bruce pulls me away. *That time, I came very close to getting stabbed, probably.*

***

Today, I am busy writing poetry. I ate some shrooms earlier, so I am in the zone, kind of out of my body, just watching my hand move uncontrollably across the paper. I look like Cousin Itt from the *Addams Family*, my long hair covering my face completely as I look down and write. This beautiful Japanese girl comes out of nowhere and sits right beside me. She is in her early twenties, I guess. A real stunner. I have not had the privilege to see many Japanese women, except on TV. Wow, she is incredibly beautiful.

I say to her, "Hello, how are you today?"

She smiles at me; she does not make a sound. She just watches me write. It is like an angel came down out of heaven. She sits there for more than two hours.

Sometimes, this improvisational poetry is like being in a dream or trance. I am not human, and the world is not still; everything just melts together to come to my pen. I am not sitting; I am flying through the cosmos. *That day, I wrote over 100 poems. The girl never spoke to me.*

***

Well, by now, it seems that every homeless person on the beach has sat or slept in my car at least once. It isn't my car anymore; it is the homeless peoples' car now. A sort of waiting room. It starts to get filthy too. I don't like it.

Tonight, Roland is again sleeping in my car, and I am sleeping close by on the sand. Bruce is about thirty feet away, also sleeping on the sand. First, the cops bust Roland in the car, then me, then Bruce. They tell us, "You can't sleep on the beach. You'll have to come with us."

So, we all go to jail. It is like a little vacation for all of us, kind of exciting. We stay overnight, and they let us go in the morning. *We even smoked a joint in the cell; Bruce had it.*

***

A few nights later, Bruce, Roland, and I decide to take a trip to Hollywood. We ride the bus, it takes forever to get there. We walk up Hollywood Boulevard, from Highland Avenue to Orange Drive. We see the footprints of the stars at the Chinese Theater and the stars on the Hollywood Walk of Fame.

I once worked for a day selling copy toner over the phone when I first arrived in LA, in the Taft Building, built in 1923 and the first high-rise at the intersection of Hollywood and Vine. Damn, Hollywood almost seems more wild than Venice, maybe a little more seedy.

Later, I say, "Hey, let's go into this liquor store, and I'll steal some beer."

Bruce and Roland look at me and say, "How are you gonna do that?"

"You two walk in and start arguing really loud. Then I'll come in after you, the cashier will only be watching you, and I can just grab a 12-pack and walk right out. They won't even see me, they'll just be watching you."

"Okay, cool. That sounds like a plan."

So, Bruce and Roland go in, and the Korean cashier gawks at only them. Then I slip in, grab the beer, and walk right out and stand outside about a half block down the street. Suddenly, the cashier comes running up to me. "Give me back the beer."

"You better get the fuck away from me, this is my beer.

I'll beat your fucking ass, motherfucker."

He turns and goes back into the liquor store and comes running back out with a hammer in his hand. He's coming straight at me. I bolt into La Cienega Boulevard, which is completely full of oncoming traffic. I am almost run over by a few cars. I look like the Heisman trophy pose, dodging cars.

Bruce and Roland come up to me after and say, "Damn, Mike, that worked pretty good."

"What do you mean, that worked good? That Korean motherfucker had a hammer. Shit, I thought I was going to get hit by a car. I ran out into fucking traffic, I'm lucky I'm not dead."

We drink the beers.

On our way back to Venice, we lose Roland, so it's just Bruce and I walking through an alley, drunk as shit.

That morning, I wake up on the bus bench at Main Street and Rose Avenue in Venice, that same bus bench in the movie *Speed*. You can see it in the background, right before the first bus blows up in the movie. I open my eyes to a 30-foot-tall ballerina clown. The statue is in a tutu, on one toe, wearing oversized white gloves and a red-nosed clown head with a hat.

Bruce tells me the next day that in the alley, I called him a name. He sheepishly whines, "Last night, Mike, you called me the N-word."

"No, I didn't. I never say that fucking word. You're full of shit. What I remember about last night is you calling me every fucking name in the book. That's what I remember."

Looking for sympathy, he says, "Yes, you did, Mike. Yes,

you did."

Well, we finally just had to agree to disagree on that one. I never say the N-word, so I know he is lying, even though I did black out.

**

Our crew never did many drugs at this time, sure we smoked weed, and I did some shrooms every once in a while, but no crack, acid, or anything else like that. Mostly, we drank Old English 40s and Cisco, usually the little bottle.

I am walking on the boardwalk, and a guy comes up to me and says, "Doses, doses, you want any doses?" For those who have never been to the street or a Grateful Dead show, doses means acid.

I say, "What you got?"

He pulls out these little pieces of paper and shows them to me. "They're five dollars a hit."

"I'll take four."

That evening, I convince Roland, Bruce, and Big Homie to do the acid with me. It takes a few hours to convince them. I believe only Bruce has done it before. I have done it twice before. None of us are too comfortable with taking it; it is just that we don't have jack-shit else to do, so what difference does it make? Eventually, we all take it and walk down to the Pier.

Roland is scared as shit. "Mike, what did you make me take? I don't feel right. Mike, I am starting to see things. Mike, I'm losing my mind."

"Just take it easy, we're all here with you. You ain't got

nothing to worry about."

"Okay, Mike, just don't go too far."

The big bad killer is scared of a little drug, I think.

At the end of the night, as we get back close to my car, Big Homie runs ahead and jumps in. He locks the doors and taunts me through the closed window. "Ha-ha, you can't get into your car. Ha-ha, you're locked out, motherfucker. I'm in control now; this is my car, bitch." He is sitting in the front passenger seat with his face almost pressed to the window. He is roaring with laughter. "You White bitch, you ain't shit, Mike. Ha-ha."

That was the most I ever heard Big Homie speak up to that point. I guess the acid really opened up his brain and his mouth.

"Ha-ha-ha," he roars.

"Come on, man, let me in. Come on, man, please. It ain't funny anymore. Come on, stop fucking around." I plead with him to open up. The only response I continue to receive is humiliating laughter. I am not in my best condition; the acid has kicked in long ago, and I have a little shorter fuse than normal. I start to get really pissed. "Get the fuck out, motherfucker, now!"

He just keeps laughing in my face. I look around and magically, at my feet, there is a metal rod. It's about two feet long. I have no idea how the hell a metal rod is just sitting there. I guess sometimes life is just how it is supposed to be.

I pick up the rod, and Bruce rushes towards me, "No, no, Mike, put that down."

"Get off me, motherfucker."

He backs up, and I rush to the car, as if I am catapulted. Big Homie's face changes; it turns from a big smile to complete surprise. I raise the bar and smash out the passenger window, right on him. He doesn't have the right to taunt me, this scared fucking kid that doesn't even speak to me, fuck him. None of the glass cuts him or hurts him; it just surprises the shit out of him. He jumps out of the car and throws me onto the hood. I go limp. I am no fool. Big Homie could kill me just with his bare hands. I am not trying to fight him. I just want him out of my car. He raises his fist. But he doesn't throw a punch. I guess he must know I don't want to fight him. Even so, he has to do something with his rage. So, he smashes out my headlight with the steel rod.

"Why not tear the whole car apart?" I say. *That was sort-of my apology, I guess, for breaking the window in his face. It was a good deal.*

He proceeds to destroy my car, piece by piece. He smashes out all the windows, rips up all the seats, flattens all the tires, rips out hoses from the engine, breaks every light, then jumps on the hood and roof until they cave in. I mean completely rips my car apart. He has such a good time, he is so happy to destroy it, and at the end, he is exhausted and panting. *I can honestly say I was happy as well. I was done with that fucking car.*

The next morning, the other homeless people come up to me and say, "Damn, what the fuck happened to your car?"

It looks like a bomb went off inside. Broken glass is everywhere, and the doors, hood, and trunk are all open. A total mess. No more waiting room for the homeless, or for Bruce to keep his fucking dog. Good, I think. I get a tow truck to haul it off; they give me five dollars. Homeless people have no position of bargaining; they have to take what they get. After that night, Big Homie and I become close friends; he really starts to like me and has my back. I like him more, too. *I never forgot that he didn't hit me.*

***

I start sleeping most of my nights at the beach lifeguard houses. They have a ramp up to the house and a little walkway that surrounds it, which is elevated by about six feet. That is just high enough for a person to sleep well. The ramp at least gives me some warning of someone walking up to me.

One night, I am sleeping and wake up quick enough to the sound of someone coming up the ramp. I immediately say, "Who's there?"

They turn around and leave. It's good to be as smart as possible when you are homeless.

***

After a little while, Roland was to go back to jail. This time, it was because of me. He got a six-month stint for assault.

I remember I was sitting at the top of this little hill by the end of Dudley Avenue, and I am pissed. Roland comes up to me and asks, "What's wrong, Mike?"

I point to James who is on his bike on the boardwalk— you remember James, he is the older homeless White guy who never talks to anyone. "Oh, that fucking James won't work with me. All I was asking is for him to buy an old bike from me."

Roland says, "Oh, I'll take care of this shit." He gets up, grabs Wolf's dog chain, and walks down the hill. First, he punches James in the face, and James falls off his bike. Then, Roland repeatedly whips him with the dog chain. James is screaming, a few of his teeth are knocked out, and he eventually loses consciousness. Roland walks right back up the hill and sits beside me.

I am in horror. "Why the fuck did you do that?"

"Mike, no one is going to fuck with you while I'm around."

"Damn man, get away from me; you're evil. You could have fucking killed him. I can't take that shit, man." Even though I appreciate Roland's loyalty, and he is still my brother, to the end, I tell him, "I'm not sure about you. I just don't know if I can continue to be your friend. Get away from me. Oh my God." I am shaking all over. I feel like I am about to pop. A bunch of cops come shortly after that and take Roland away.

I only saw Roland two more times after that. I always thought I was to blame for the beating James took. And in some way, it was my fault Roland went to jail. I should've never said anything. They took James away in an ambulance, and I never saw him again.

***

As the summer wears down, less people are visiting Venice. Less people, less poems, less money. It is getting harder and harder to make it on the beach. I can't take it.

Roland was the glue that held us all together; now he is gone. It isn't much fun anymore. Bruce and I begin to fight all the time. I find it hard to get enough to eat. I have a food stamp card that lasts about two weeks out of a month. So, for two weeks, sometimes, I am hungry. I call my mom and ask for help. She sends me $100 or more to get by. My mother is always in my corner. I can go home to Colorado and live with her, anytime, if I want. But I just can't do it. I have to find the reason why I came to California.

Oakwood Ghost Town

On this dreary autumn day, I am standing in a food line for free lunch at a homeless shelter. I rarely do this; it is just a tough day, I have to get something to eat. I am hungry. As I stand in line, a car slowly drives by and pulls over. Out jumps Ethan, the waiter I had worked with at Michael's. Ethan is a cool White guy, who has been really nice to me.

"Hey, Mike, what are you up to?"

"Oh, just trying to get something to eat."

"Hey, why don't you come over to my house with me? I've got food at my place. I haven't seen you in forever; we can get a chance to talk. Besides, I was just about to make lunch for my girl, anyway. What about it, you want to come over and have a beer? I live right around the corner. We got a cool place."

"Okay, I guess so. If it's no trouble. Damn, I haven't seen you in forever. How have you been?"

"Good. Come on, hop in my car."

I get in, and we drive about two blocks to his house. A pretty nice place, right in the hood. The neighborhood is called Oakwood, aka Ghost Town. Oakwood is a half-square mile section west of Lincoln Boulevard. In the early 1900s, Abbot Kinney hired Black people to construct the canals in Venice. Oakwood used to be a segregated community. At one point, it was the only place in Los Angeles where Black people could own property. For a while, it was a fenced-off area for Blacks, Italians, and

Mexicans to buy homes. In the 1940s, the population of Black people tripled; the community was completely surrounded by White neighborhoods. In the 1950s, Venice was known as the Ghetto by the Sea and as a result, Oakwood's cheap housing prices attracted young counterculture artists and poor European immigrants. The neighborhood maintained a Black working-class population; and made it also relatively easy for Mexicans to settle in. It is a majority Black neighborhood today.

I walk into the house with Ethan. His girlfriend welcomes me right away. Her name is Betty. She is very sweet and asks if I want a beer. I am so shocked. Wow, this is what a roof over your head looks like, I comically think. About five minutes after I sit on the couch, a goofy looking White guy with a mohawk comes in. I think, who the fuck is this guy?

"Hi, my name is Jack."

I get up and shake his hand. "Nice to meet you, Jack. My name is Mike."

We all sit and smoke a joint and have a few beers. Damn, I haven't talked to this many White people in a minute. Betty also waits tables, and Ethan and her are looking for a house of their own. They are to be married soon. Jack is an artist studying at Parsons Art School which is one of the finest art schools in all of California. His paintings are hung up all over the house. Jack's father had once been a billionaire, so he tells me, and was friends with Clint Eastwood in Monterey County; Clint used to tuck Jack in at night sometimes when he was a little boy. *In the time I knew him, Jack was a really interesting person. We became very close; he actually inspired me to be a better artist.*

So, after we talk for a couple of hours, I say, "Well, I got to get going."

Ethan says, "Mike, why don't you just crash here for the night? Do you have a sleeping bag?"

"Yes, but it's back at the beach."

"Oh, don't worry about it, we have some extra blankets you can use."

Betty says, "Yeah, just crash here. We have an empty room if you don't mind sleeping on the floor."

"No, that's okay. I'm fine. I gotta go."

They all three insist I stay the night.

So eventually, I say, "Okay."

Later that evening, in walk a woman and her small son. Her name is Jessica and her son's name is Mattie. The house is hers, and Jack is her younger brother. Mattie is about four years old; he is biracial, half-White, half-Black. When I first see Mattie, I immediately think, wow, what a beautiful child, just a ray of sunshine. *Me and Mattie went on to become great friends. I watched out for him like he was my own son.* Jessica is White and American Indian; she is a very nice lady, kind of a hippie girl. She graduated from UCLA, and once, traveled with the Grateful Dead for an entire summer, selling jewelry she made. She now works as an aid counselor for poor people.

Ethan introduces me. "Jessica, this is Mike. I used to work with him at Michael's."

We exchange greetings.

Mattie comes up to me. "Who are you? Why are you here in our house? Mom, what is this guy doing here?"

"Now, Mattie, leave him alone and get ready to eat. Mike, would you like to have dinner with us?" She has brought home chicken for the house. *I think it was El Pollo Loco, it might have been KFC.*

"Only if you have enough. I don't want to put you out."

"Oh, don't worry, we have plenty."

Wow, what it is to have people be kind to you.

For the first time in quite a while, I sleep with a roof over my head. I guess the first step up from the bottom is always a long climb. I am tossing and turning all night. I trust no one. Part of me, by this time, is a little wild. I have now become street, I understand how to survive in the hood, I am not afraid. My attitude is not of anger, more of confidence. I understand how to live in LA and Venice. This is exactly where I want to be. *I loved Venice Beach, and I still do. Although, I did think, why the heck would these White people let me spend the night in their house? They don't even know me. I could be a bad person. And I was a little bad, anyway. A homeless guy. That was how Venice Beach was, I learned. People were so nice sometimes. It certainly made me become nicer the longer I lived there.*

I wake up early the next morning to leave quietly before anyone else is up. As I am almost at the door, Jessica says, "Mike, do you want a cup of coffee?"

I look over, and she is standing there, sunshine radiating all around her. She is so beautiful. "Sure, okay."

We sit and drink coffee and talk. She is a real LA woman, a California woman. I make sure not to flirt or show her that I think she is attractive. After all, I barely met her. Jack comes into the kitchen next, gets himself a cup, and sits by me and starts talking. I have a feeling he thinks I am cool. Then, Ethan comes in and gets a cup.

Jessica says, "Hey, if you want to rent the empty room, you can. No one's in there. Would you like to stay?"

I hide my jubilance. "Yes, that would be great. Thank you very much. I really appreciate it so much."

So, I walk to the beach, which is only four blocks away to get my belongings from behind the synagogue and move into my new room that very day. The house has five bedrooms: Ethan and Betty have their room, Jack has his room, Mattie has his own room, and Jessica's room is right next to his. There is only one bathroom, which is a hassle sometimes. It is a warm home, though. A real place of love, I think. It has a little front yard with big bushes along Brooks Avenue. They are just tall enough so that no one can look inside the house, which is nice. In the back is a large yard with a covered patio and an alleyway further out. *I remember there was an old Karmann Ghia car in the back yard that Jessica left there when it died. You know, we should have been afraid to live in the hood, but no one ever came through the back gate, not once.*

Jessica is a progressive democrat who teaches me so much about the real world. I am from Colorado and was born in Texas, where it seemed to me that everyone was living okay. In the real world, people are not okay, they have to heal, they have to eat, they have to have a roof over their heads. I had been living in a fantasy world, where I thought I was the only one suffering. *Jessica's mission was, and probably still is, to be a good human being and to treat others like good human beings. She worked to see that there were none less fortunate, there were only people living in harmony. She was my teacher and helped me become, politically, who I am today.*

I enjoy hearing Jessica's point of view. I enjoy being around her. We both despise George HW Bush, so we talk about Bill Clinton and how he seems like the answer. Wasn't Clinton's wife involved as well? I guess he would be a good president, if he isn't too corrupt, him and his wife. Jessica and I talk politics and how to change the world for the better. *I believe I inspired her as much as she inspired me.*

***

Lucky enough, I quickly get a job waiting tables at a restaurant only a block and a half away from the house; it is called the Sculpture Gardens, located at 1031 Abbot Kinney Boulevard. Right in the century-old artistic neighborhood of Abbot Kinney Boulevard; GQ Magazine once defined Abbot Kinney Boulevard as "The Coolest Block In America." The Sculpture Gardens is part of a two-block complex named Venice Place; it is part restaurant, part garden, and part plant shop. It has a small kitchen house in the back. There is this huge garden, like a Japanese zen garden, with a koi pond and an actual little stream rolling down a small hill. A real paradise. Some of the restaurant tables even sit in the garden. There is a 50-car parking lot, with an incoming gate on Electric Avenue and an outgoing gate on Westminster Avenue, at the far south end of the property; to get out of this gate requires a token. The property is bordered on the hood by Electric Avenue; for added protection there is a ten-foot tall fence covered by a thick hedge that is about six feet wide. The compound is a really cool and safe place in Venice.

In the front of Venice Place, on Abbot Kinney Boulevard, there is a watch shop, a five-star restaurant called Joe's, another healthy restaurant called A Votre Santé, a coffee shop, and then the Sculpture Gardens. Behind Joe's and A Votre Santé are two houses. The guys who own the watch shop live in one of the houses. One of them is Vidal Sassoon's nephew. In the other house, a potter named Bob rents the basement as his studio. He and I sometimes go and play pool; he gave me some really nice ceramic vases. The upper floor is empty, Jerry rents it out as office space occasionally. Above A Votre Santé is an office where people sell watches over the phone; there are usually three or four people working there. Right across the hall from this office is where Hutch, from *Starsky and Hutch*, lived in the show; that was his apartment. Across Abbot Kinney Boulevard is Westminster Avenue Elementary School.

Venice Place and the Sculpture Gardens are owned by an older Jewish man named Jerry. He is the salt of the earth; a very good, rich man. He is in his upper 60s, although he has the activity level of someone who is 18. Jerry lives in Brentwood and has this incredible house; there is a tall hill in his backyard and a huge pond. He has made his long professional career as a psychiatrist. *Part of me always thought he was looking at me as a subject.* I believe he was born in LA, and his father bought the land where Venice Place now is, years before, when it was owned by the railroad. In fact, the street behind the property, Electric Avenue, still has railroad tracks on it.

At my first job interview with Jerry, he is twitching

around and can't sit still, and I think, wow, this is the guy who owns all this place. *I found out through time that Jerry was one of the wisest men I would ever meet. I heard that he passed away a few years back. I hold him in great honor for the man his life proved he was, for the genuine care he demonstrated toward so many.*

***

Everything is going great. I am really living it up now, no more homeless bullshit. I am making it. I wait tables in the day or night, and always come home to a lively household. We often sit down and have a chat over a joint. What's happening in the world? What have you heard? It is all good.

Jessica and Ethan have some great friends, and I begin to go to parties with them, LA parties, full of UCLA alumni and hippie intellectuals. I fit in pretty well, but I don't quite meet the mark for some of them. I don't care. I am a hippie and learning to be an intellectual. If I'm not smart enough, I ask, "What's your dream?" Sometimes, I am the life of the party. There is a lawyer; his name is Ben. He graduated from UCLA, same as Jessica, and has a law office right on the Venice boardwalk. A cool young White dude who is open to discussion other than just the LA point of view. *I remember late one night at a party at his house, I was blasting his expensive stereo equipment—damn, it was loud. He didn't say anything. I made some good friends while I was living on Brooks Avenue.*

***

One day, I get the good idea to buy a pool table and put it out on the back porch. I look in the newspaper and find one. It isn't high quality, it is just enough. What a great investment; we play for hours. Jack installs some speakers out on the patio, now it's always a party. I get to know Jack a lot more, just by playing pool almost every night. He has the best music on vinyl records, old school stuff, like James Brown, Sly and the Family Stone, Marvin Gaye, Al Green, The Stylistics; what a party.

***

After a month, when Jessica and I are off from work, we are sitting and talking, and I slowly reach over to give her a kiss. *No, I asked her before I did it.* "Can I give you a kiss?"

She says yes, and that is the beginning of our relationship. We are a good couple. Everybody likes it in the house, even her brother. I fall in love with Jessica; she is my rock. I love her very much. Now I have a house, a job, and a girlfriend. Damn, I am coming up quick.

***

A few months pass, and I am walking to the beach. Bruce is sitting in a pagoda with a few people. "What's up, Bruce? How have you been?"

"Doing okay, Mike. I can't complain." Bruce introduces me to the young guy sitting next to him. "This is Mike. He's

OG."

The kid looks at me with such high regard. I am so proud to have earned OG status from Bruce. Even if he might have been bullshitting. Heck, I am not sure I would say that he is OG. Oh, for those that don't know what OG means, it means original gangster.

Bruce says, "Damn, Mike, I thought you went back to Colorado."

"No, I am living over on Brooks Avenue now. Renting a room in this house. Really cool people I live with. You should come by some time."

"Okay, Mike, I will."

After we sit there for about thirty minutes talking, I say, "Hey, what are you doing now? Do you like to play pool? I bought an old pool table for the back porch, and it is nice just to hang out back there. You want to go?" *I knew that was a mistake. I just wanted to see one of my old beach friends, and I had a weak moment.*

Of course, Bruce is too loud and obnoxious at the house. I think he scares all my roommates. He starts coming over to the house whenever he wants. I keep him in line and boot his ass out if he gets too crazy, he knows that. It happens a couple of times that I have to kick him out. One time, I even put a pool cue to his neck. He tries to flirt with Jessica, and I am crazy, especially about Jessica.

***

One great day, my brother and his wife visit me. Jessica and I meet them for lunch in Marina Del Rey. It is so cool to be in California with my brother. He has always been my best friend; he always will be. We let each other be our own selves.

***

Today, Jessica wants to introduce me to an older White couple that she really likes. They live about a block down Brooks Avenue. We walk over to their house and stay for lunch. The older guy, Peter, was a professor at Santa Monica College for years and is now retired. There are books everywhere throughout the apartment. I start to go over and visit him a lot. He is so knowledgeable about every subject. So polite and patient. Peter is the first person to ever mention Rastafari and Haile Selassie to me.

***

Ethan and Betty have a dog, he stays out in the backyard in the day and comes in the house at night. California summers are tough on dogs because of fleas. After a short while, we have fleas all over our house. They are eating Jack alive. Finally, Jessica and I have to flea bomb the house, all of us have to leave for a few hours. At least those little pesky, bastards are gone.

***

It is my day to watch Mattie. I am off work, and he has no school. So we decide to go to the beach, have some lunch, and walk around. Whenever I am out with him, I hold his hand the entire time. He is so rambunctious, though; he often tries to break away and run. When I take him out onto the sand, he runs all he wants. I fake wrestle with him, or tickle him, and he bursts into laughter.

A while back, I got a big boombox for cheap. Sometimes, I carry it with me on the boardwalk, and today I brought it with us. At the end of our very cool day, Mattie and I are walking toward home, he is sitting on my shoulders, and the boombox is blasting *Bring tha Noize* from the album *Apocalypse 91… The Enemy Strikes Black* by Public Enemy. All the passing people on the boardwalk just smile at us.

***

It is getting close to Christmas, Jessica and I go to get a tree. She has some ornaments, but we get even more. Mattie helps us decorate the tree, he is so excited that Santa is coming. On Christmas Eve, he will not go to sleep, so Jessica takes him into her room and shuts the door. He finally nods off.

In the morning, he rushes out to see what Santa brought him. There are a ton of presents. Then, I tell him there is another surprise on the patio. He sprints out, and there is a little rabbit. I built the rabbit a hutch, as well. Mattie jumps up and down, hollering with glee. I give him the rabbit to hold, but it scratches his arm. After that, Mattie doesn't like the rabbit so much anymore.

***

Jessica pushes me to take my script to Oliver Stone. I do some research and find out his office is in Venice. I write down the address and walk to his office to try and meet him. On the way, I wonder if my script is good enough. I have my doubts.

When I enter the office, a receptionist greets me. "Hello, how can I assist you?"

"Is this the office of Oliver Stone?"

"Yes, it is. Do you have an appointment with Mr. Stone?"

"No, I do not. I have a script that I wanted to share with him. Would he be available to meet with me for a few minutes?"

"Well, he is very busy today. If you like, I can take the script and make sure he gets it. Would you like to leave a copy with me?"

"Oh, no. That's okay. I will come back when he is not so busy. Thank you for your time."

I walk out knowing I have no intention of going back. The script is so personal to me that there is no way I can leave it with someone else. Hell, I don't even have a copy, I only have the original. *I never did take the script to him, I should have, I just didn't. Maybe I was scared.*

***

Today, Ethan, Betty, Jessica, and I go to Sunset Beach. Ethan is going to teach me how to surf. I think it will be fun. The beach is located at the end of Sunset Boulevard, where the waves break on the south and west rolls.

Ethan says, "Sunset Beach is the best place for you to learn to surf."

Well, I try to get up many times, Ethan is patient with me, but I don't really think my heart is in it. If you want to know the truth, I just want to sit on the beach with Jessica. Maybe make-out a little bit. *So, I was not successful in becoming a surfer that day. The girls and I sat and watched Ethan surf.*

***

Jessica, Mattie, and I go to the La Brea Tar Pits; there are more than 100 pits with the tar-preserved bones of trapped animals. On the grounds of the park are life-sized models of prehistoric animals. It's pretty cool.

***

Tonight, Jessica and I are going to play pool at a bar in Culver City. Coming with us are Big Homie, David and his girlfriend, and one of Jessica's friends. You remember David, he is the young Black kid from the beach who is too young to be homeless. He now has short dreads and is about 23 years old. He likes to hang out at the house sometimes. We are pretty good friends. His girlfriend is a big, White girl; she has a car and would drive us around. So, we're all at this bar playing pool. We have been playing for a while just against each other. I go over and put my quarters up on another table; I can see that this table has the best players. It is three games before my turn, so I go back to talk to Jessica. Finally, when it's my turn, I put my quarters in and rack them up.

Just as my opponent is about to break, another guy comes up and says to me, "No, man, it's my turn."

"No, dude, I waited three games. I was watching the whole time. I'm up next. I just racked."

"No, you aren't, so that's it. It's my game."

"No, it isn't."

"What are you going to do about it?" The guy pushes me.

I push him back. Boom, here we go fighting. I end up having to fight three guys; they just keep coming at me. It is crazy; the whole bar starts fighting. I look over, and Big Homie has about three guys coming at him, too. He is swinging wildly. At least Homie is up for a squabble, I know that. After fighting my third guy, I say fuck this and grab an empty bottle. If anybody comes at me again I am going to crack them on the head. Then I see a couple of them grab empty bottles, too. Jessica takes over at this point and screams to get us out of there. We all go running out.

***

For a while, it is the best of both worlds. I have my house friends, and I have my beach friends. I am respected in both places. They are from two completely different crowds, so I am very cautious about introducing them to each other; I do not want to fuck up my situation.

***

The Rodney King trial is drawing to an end in Simi Valley; the trial has been moved from LA County out to the Whitest place they can find. Of course, the officers will still be found guilty—our eyes do not lie, even if our judicial system does. The verdict comes in on April 29, 1992, the jury of nine White, one Latino, one biracial, one Asian, acquits all four officers of assault and three of the four of using excessive force.

The entire city of Los Angeles collectively groans, "What the fuck?"

Outside the courthouse, director John Singleton says, "By having this verdict, what these people done, they lit the fuse to a bomb."

I am down at the beach that day, and I foolishly say to Bruce and some others, "I bet nothing happens. LA ain't got no heart."

That day, LA began to burn. I had greatly underestimated the veracity of neglected anger. Black people had experienced these types of illegal beatings by corrupt police officers for a long time. Shit, Daryl Gates, the chief of the LAPD from 1978 to 1992, had promoted this type of abuse. In a May 1982 interview with the Los Angeles Times, Gates famously remarked on the use of choke holds by police: "We may be finding that in some Blacks when [it] is applied, the veins or arteries do not open up as fast as they do in normal people." At the time of the 1992 rebellion, 47 percent of Black men and teenagers in Los Angeles were classified by law enforcement authorities as gang members.

I remember at first the riot was just burning in South Central, then Hollywood, then Long Beach, and then other areas. We stayed in our house and watched TV. If I had been out on the street, I could have been killed just for having White skin. I stayed my ass indoors. Though

I did wish I could loot a nice TV, too.

About ten minutes after the verdict was announced, crowds gathered at the Pay-Less Liquor and Deli on Florence Avenue in South Central. Some protesters went to LAPD headquarters, smashing windows and chanting "No Justice, No Peace." Others looted stores at the intersection of Florence and Normandie or attacked motorists. A news helicopter captured the beating of White truck driver Reginald Denny by a group of Black men.

As the sun went down, the mass looting and arson began. Stores were ransacked and burned. Much of the violence targeted the immigrant communities of Koreatown and Pico-Union. Tensions between Black and Korean residents had increased since the year before, when—two weeks after Rodney King's assault—Black ninth-grader Latasha Harlins was fatally shot by a Korean storeowner over a $1.79 bottle of orange juice. It was later discovered Harlins was clutching money to pay for the juice when she was killed. Harlins's killer, Soon Ja Du, received probation, community service, and a five-hundred-dollar fine. A member of the Bloods explained. "This riot is about all the homeboys murdered by the police, about the little sister killed by the Koreans, about twenty-seven years of oppression, Rodney King was just the trigger.

Now, it seems the entire city is burning; it is a very dangerous situation. It feels like anarchy is going to break out, and people will just start rushing into your home. The second night of the riots, a fire is lit in the intersection right outside our house, at Brooks Avenue and 4th Avenue; it is a six-foot-tall pile of burning stuff. *That was pretty crazy.*

The same night, Jessica, Jack, and I step onto the back patio to have a smoke, and this White guy who has come through our front gate, runs along the side of the house into our backyard and onto the patio.

"Oh, man, they are chasing after me. Can you hide me?" he says.

I am sitting and jump up. "Who the fuck are you? Fuck no, we can't hide you, get the fuck out of here. Hit it. You got to go, fucker." Jessica lets him go out the back gate. I know that was mean of me, not to help him, but I don't know the guy. It is a very scary time. Jessica tells me later that she thought I was mean to do that.

The next night, we hear loud sirens coming into our neighborhood. I'm like, what the heck is going on, so I go creeping out into the front yard and hide behind the bushes. As I wait, I see a cop car driving real slow. There is someone on a loudspeaker saying, "As of now, your neighborhood and all of Venice is under Martial Law. You should remain in your homes, until further notice. If you do not comply, you will be subject to being arrested or shot."

Right behind the police car are about twenty US Army trucks full of soldiers with M16s between their knees; they just keep coming by, one after the other. I run back inside. We soon learn that Venice is under a dusk-to-dawn curfew. You cannot go out after dark. If you are out after dark, you can be shot on sight. Soldiers begin to walk two by two, day and night, along Brooks Avenue and throughout Venice. Even the gangsters stay inside after dark. Soldiers can be much more dangerous than gangsters. It is strange to be walking through an American neighborhood and have two soldiers pass you with M16 rifles.

After the riots, certain neighborhoods are just gutted. Now people have to go miles away to get basic needs. Violence based on one's skin is ridiculous. Damn, Reginald Denny isn't one of the officers that beat Rodney King. Racism in all forms is ignorance. Of course, poverty and economic restrictions will eventually drive anybody crazy. I am just a White guy who has nothing to do with the suffering, but that uncontrollable crowd would have busted me in the head with a brick. For a moment, it seems all White people in LA are afraid. *I always thought it was strange though that the people were burning down their own neighborhood stores. Why not go to someone else's neighborhood and take their shit?* I know a lot of Black people who also think the riots are a waste; destroying your own neighborhood, it makes no sense. I mean, I can't stand the cops either. I just don't want to start burning shit down to prove it.

Attorney General William Barr invoked the Insurrection Act to quickly organize the federal force, which consisted of FBI and Border Patrol Agents, special SWAT teams, US Marshals, and prison riot squads, in addition to thousands of Marines and Army soldiers.

On May 1, as the city is burning, Rodney King gives a news conference. He says, "I just want to say—you know— can we, can we all get along? Can we, can we get along?"

I am like fuck that. Part of me thinks, we don't need no water, let the motherfucker burn.

The rioting lasts six days; 64 people die, including nine shot by police and one by the National Guard. Of those killed, 28 are Black, 19 are Latino, 15 are White, and 2 are

Asian; no soldiers or police die. Also, 2,383 people are injured, 3,600 fires set, and 1,100 buildings destroyed; property damage is at $1 billion. The riots only stop when 10,072 California National Guard and 2,000 US military troops, and federal law enforcement agencies are deployed. In total, more than twenty thousand law enforcement officers and soldiers arrest 16,291 people. Of those arrested during the riots, 36 percent were Blacks and 51 percent were Latinos. It is the first significant military occupation of LA by federal troops since the 1894 Pullman Strike, and also the first federal military intervention in an American city since the riots in 1968 due to the Martin Luther King assassination. Federal troops do not stand down until May 9; some National Guard soldiers remain as late as May 27.

The riots taught me one big lesson about Los Angeles: It had mad heart and a lot of it.

***

After being locked in my house for a few weeks because of the riots, I walk to the beach and see Big Homie and Bruce in a pagoda talking with a few other people. We say hello and start to reminisce on some of our old stories, laughing and having a great time. One of the people sitting with us is this guy that I don't know.

He keeps interrupting. "I will outsmoke any of you."

"That's a bold statement," I say.

Bruce agrees. "Do you know who the fuck you're talking to, you must be fucking crazy."

"No. No one can outsmoke me. You all are old, and I

know I can outsmoke all of you." The guy goes on and on about his extreme prowess on every subject.

I start to get a little annoyed. "Hey, man, we are old friends, and we haven't seen each other in a while. Can you just sit down and let us talk? You keep interrupting. Can I just speak with my friends?"

He doesn't even acknowledge my existence and just keeps on. "I know I can kick all your asses, too. Nobody can beat me."

After a few minutes, I stand up and tell him, "Okay, that's it, either you shut the fuck up and sit the fuck down, or you got to go. Which one is it going to be?" He barely glances at me, sits there, and starts to talk about another subject. I think, damn, my friends and I can't even have a fucking conversation because of this loud dude. So I say, "That's it, motherfucker. You hit it right now, or I am going to kick your motherfucking ass, right here. Understand? Get to stepping, motherfucker. Now. Don't say shit, just get the fuck up and leave. Let's go, fucker. I ain't joking. Hit it."

He mumbles something, and I kind of move over even closer toward him. Finally, he gets up and hastily walks away.

Bruce smiles. "Damn, Mike, for a minute there, I thought he was going to kick your fucking ass, until you pulled that Crip walk on him. He got to fucking stepping after that."

Big Homie laughs. "Shit yeah, I saw that, too. Damn, Mike, you're one crazy motherfucker."

***

Today, Jessica, Jack, Mattie, and I are off to spend the day at the beach. Jessica drives us to Manhattan Beach by the pier. It is beautiful. We pack a lunch, pick up some beer, and put ice over it in a cooler. It is a wonderful day. Jessica is always so nice, she is a pleasure to be with.

Jack has this skimboard. Skimboarding is an activity that was born in the late 1920s when Laguna Beach lifeguards would use thin pieces of wood to slide on the flat water along the sand. Jack is good at it. To do it, you start running and drop your board flat out in front of you on the thin coat of water; you have to refrain from just hopping straight on top because you will fall, and it will hurt. Jack tells me, "Try to run onto the board by placing your lead foot toward the front of the board first and then following with the back foot. Then you won't lose your speed as you jump on."

I try to do it many times. I about break my hip. Finally, I just say, fuck it.

***

Saturday, Jessica and I attend the wedding of one of her friends at Will Rogers Beach. It is a beautiful ceremony. *I remember sitting there that day thinking, would Jessica and I ever be doing this? Would we ever get married? I came to the conclusion, no. She didn't seem like the marrying type. I guess sometimes, I felt more like her son than her boyfriend, for some reason. She was just always in control, and I was just a plaything for her, unless the shit hit the fan and she wanted me to be in control. It's hard to not be an equal to the one you love.*

***

Today, Jessica and I are on the boardwalk to have lunch at The Sidewalk Cafe, it is a great time. On our way back to the house, we see these two guys fighting. A White dude and a Latino guy. It is crazy, like bare-knuckles boxing, neither can get the best of the other one. They just keep hitting each other in the face, eventually one guy has a deep cut open up over his eye. I think you can see the bone. He has blood running down his face. He still will not go down.

Jessica tells me, "Mike, break it up. Stop them."

"I ain't stopping nothing. They will turn on me, and I'll have to fight. I'm not getting involved."

She is so disappointed in me. She says she has lost respect for me and that I am not a peaceful man.

***

Just down from our house on Brooks Avenue, whenever I walk to the store by the New Bethel Baptist Church at 503 Brooks Avenue, every guy on the sidewalk tries to sell me crack. They say, "What you need? What you need?"

The entire time I lived in Venice, if the cops drove by when I walked down the street, they would just stare at me. They wouldn't even acknowledge the fact that the same fucking guy was on the same fucking corner every day selling crack. Good ol' George HW Bush was doing his best to work with the Medellín Cartel and Bill Clinton to pump that shit in as fast as possible. The LAPD turned a blind eye to the crack epidemic, at least in Oakwood.

For the better part of a decade, a drug ring sold tons of cocaine to the Crips and Bloods street gangs of Los Angeles and funneled millions in drug profits to a Latin American guerrilla army run by the U.S. Central Intelligence Agency, a San Jose Mercury News investigation found. This drug network opened the first pipeline between Colombia's cocaine cartels and the Black neighborhoods of Los Angeles, a city now known as the crack capital of the world.

***

One evening, Jack pulls me into his room. "Mike, I want to smoke some crack tonight."

I have never done any of that before and am a little surprised he would ask me to smoke with him. I never saw him smoke crack, either.

"Mike, if I go out and try to buy it, they will rip me off. But, if you go, they will give you what you pay for. Will you go get it?"

"Why do you want to smoke crack? What's up?"

"Oh, it will be fun. It can't be that bad."

Reluctantly, I say, "Okay, I'll go get it." I buy about $20 of crack and smoke it all with Jack. *That was the first and only time Jack and I ever smoked crack together.*

***

A few weeks later, we're all out back playing pool, talking, trying to think of something to do that will be really fun, and Jessica says, "Let's go to Disneyland on acid."

I say, "That'd be cool. I'll go."

Everybody else in the house agrees. *So, we all went to*

Disneyland on acid.

***

Another night, Jessica and I go to the Sunset Strip bar hopping. We go to the Whisky A Go-Go and see some big hair bands. Then to the Roxy for a drink. I have never seen so much spiked hair in my life.

***

As time passes, I am sad to say I begin to not trust Jessica. I suspect she is cheating on me. I know I am paranoid having just come from the streets; and I know I am not great about being patient. Maybe it is my lack of self-confidence, maybe it is this, maybe it is that.

I start driving her crazy with all my questions. "Where were you, who were you with, are you cheating on me?"

The answer is always no. Jessica is cool; there is just this small side of her that seems to be deceptive. It drives me crazy, and I am driving her crazy. I take full responsibility for this drama; I am the cause of the misunderstanding. *Today, I would only say maybe I was wrong; maybe it really was Jessica. Ultimately, if you can't trust someone, you know you have to leave.*

***

Today, Jessica and I are off to Las Vegas to see two shows of the Grateful Dead. We are trying hard to make it work, and this will be a good break from being in Venice.

There are three cars full of friends going with us. We have tickets for Friday and Saturday. On Thursday night, we all go to a pig roast. Of course, I am on pins and needles trying to keep an eye on Jessica. I am kind of a mess; I'm sprung. At most parties now, I find myself going off alone and just sitting there because I have no one to talk to. Blah, blah, blah, they all go on. I am starting to pass the talk and think of action. These White hippie intellectuals are boring compared to the homeless.

We get up the next day and go to the first show at the Sam Boyd Silver Bowl at UNLV. It is May 29, 1992. On the way, Jessica hands me a hit of acid; I take it. As we walk into the stadium, there are people all around selling jewelry, clothes, hats, all kinds of things. The magic bus of hippies has definitely arrived. The people are all so colorful, and they move a certain way. I love it. They have long hair, dreadlocks, and there are some real beautiful women. I enjoy the atmosphere very much.

The Steve Miller Band is the opening band. They are great. As the Grateful Dead come on to the stage, my mind is opened. I am not the biggest fan of the Dead; on this day though, they are amazing. Mickey Hart is playing the drums exactly with the strikes of lightning bouncing off the mountains in the background. You can even hear the crowd oohing and aahing all over the place. It is like going to a choreographed 4th of July show. *I said that day and have ever since, I believe God came to the show.*

On the second day, about half-way through the show, this beautiful girl sits next to me. There are a lot of empty seats around, but this girl decides to sit next to me. Jessica is on my other side. I can sense she doesn't like it. I don't even talk to the girl; she just sits there for about thirty minutes, and then she leaves. After that, Jessica and I are over. Secretly, I am so happy the girl came to sit by me. Jessica is lucky to be dating me, and if she is cheating on me, then at least she knows beautiful women want to be with me. So, I think, forget Jessica; she is becoming too much drama. I know that I have to leave. When we get back to Venice from Vegas, Jessica tells me I need to find another place.

The next day, I talk to Jerry, the owner of Venice Place. I ask him if we can go to lunch. He drives me in his Mercedes 450SL to a place he knows in Marina Del Rey. It is very nice, with a panoramic view of the marina. Jerry tells me about how he has started seeing a new lady.

I listen and at the end of discussing the subject, I ask him, "Are you getting any pussy?"

"No."

"If you aren't getting any pussy, don't be giving any money."

He looks at me like I have a third eye. I assume he thinks, who the hell is this kid? How can he be this way with me? *While I thought he liked the fact that I told the straight truth, as I saw it at that time, I have learned much more since then. Now, I would never say some of the things I said back then.*

We continue our lunch, just two buddies having a meal. As we drive back to Venice Place, I ask him, "Hey, Jerry, isn't there an apartment above the Sculpture Gardens?"

"Yes."

"Could I see it?"

"Oh, no one lives up there."

"Can I see it, though?"

"Okay. But I don't want to rent it to anyone."

He shows me the apartment. It is on the second story, directly above the Sculpture Gardens restaurant, with its own private entrance on the outside of the building. It is wonderful. As you enter and walk to the top of the stairs, on the left is a kitchen with a little table to sit and eat by the window, a bathroom with a clawfoot tub surrounded by a shower curtain, a porcelain sink, and another tiny room that is just the right size for a futon. The windows in the kitchen and bathroom look out over the Sculpture Gardens patio and parking lot, out to the Oakwood hood. There is a door into the kitchen, so this side of the loft is almost like a little one-bedroom apartment by itself. If you turn right at the top of the stairs, there is a large room with eight-foot ceilings; a detailed beach scene is painted on all the walls and the ceiling. I am stunned by this room, someone must have taken a long time to paint all this, there are even little people painted everywhere having fun. It is so Venice Beach. If you walk out a back door in this room, toward the front of the restaurant, there is a really cool outside patio, which looks right down on Abbot Kinney Boulevard. Part of the roof is on a slant, so they have built wood stands; it is so cool, kind of like a little amphitheater.

After the loft tour, Jerry and I sit in the Sculpture Gardens. "Jerry, if you help me, I'll help you. I will watch over this entire place and make sure everything is okay. Besides, it would be good to have someone on site. I will watch over it like it was my own. What do you say, Jerry? Please, can I rent it?"

He insists he does not want to rent it to anyone. Apparently someone once lived up there, and it didn't work out.

I keep at him, "Jerry, me and my girlfriend are breaking up, and she wants me out. I don't have anywhere to go. Can you help me out?"

After some real negotiating, or begging on my part, he finally agrees, "Okay then, you will need to pay $800 a month to rent the apartment. Of course, you'll continue to work in the restaurant downstairs for lunch and dinner shifts. Also, I want you to work with Emma, in the plant shop, you'll need to assist her with watering and the maintenance of all the plants. You will also be responsible for taking the parking lot tokens to the restaurants every day, or as much as needed, so that their customers can get out of the parking lot gate. The restaurants will pay you for the tokens at $1 each. Every Tuesday when I come by, I will get the money. Last thing, I want you to work with Miguel to maintain the property, as well."

"Okay, no problem, Jerry. That will be fine. I'll do good work. Thank you so much. You are a good man. I appreciate it so much. I won't let you down."

He smiles. "You better not."

I go home from the meeting so happy. I have found my way again It seems I am always finding my way; of course, with the help of others. I immediately tell Jessica I have found another place and will be leaving tomorrow. The next day, I ask Jack to help me move my pool table, and off I go. He thinks my new apartment is the greatest. He starts stopping by for unannounced visits, just to say hey. I like my friends to do that.

This change is good for both Jessica and me. It probably hurts Mattie the most, for which I am sorry. Jessica, Jack, and I have all come to the understanding that life spent in drama is wasted days. Growth is a good thing.

King Of Venice

Now, I have a spot. Wow, it is amazing. I am the King of Venice. I am always so lucky. God always blesses me. Maybe it has a little to do with the fact that I am talented and cool. I do trust in God, that is what I attribute to my survival. Positivity and having no fear will take you a long way. When I was 17, I got smashed between two cars on a little Suzuki TS 125 motorcycle. It actually bent the motorcycle in half. This lady came over a hill right before the stoplight and slammed me from behind into the car in front. She hit me so hard, both my legs went flying straight up into the air. After the crash, one leg was on each car. The cop that came told me I should be dead. I only had one little scratch on my leg. I have always been lucky or blessed. Think of it: a short while ago, I was sleeping at the lifeguard house to protect myself, and now, I was in control of two blocks in Venice, California, which were only two and a half blocks from the boardwalk. It's paradise.

The first night I sleep in the loft apartment, I am wide awake almost the entire night. I think I hear a gunshot outside. I finally fall asleep and dream that I am a superhero. Life is divine. Have you ever gone to sleep listening to waves? *It was so beautiful, I slept like a baby almost every night.*

***

Jack and I put the pool table out on my patio; of

course, the rain eventually ruins it. When it gets too worn out, I finally set it out on the corner of Electric Avenue and Broadway Street, it is gone in ten minutes. It is damn good for a while, though, out on the patio. In the beginning, I play pool by myself and listen to the crashing ocean waves. Then, Jack comes over and plays. He starts bringing his college friends, too. My apartment becomes the party zone.

***

Joe's restaurant has valet parking. There is a Brazilian guy named Gabriel who is the parking attendant. He works almost every night. He is from Santos, on the island of São Vicente, 14 miles south of Sao Paulo, on the coast. Pele played for Santos at age 15, he was Santos's all-time top goalscorer and the only player to ever win three World Cups in 1958, 1962, and 1970. Gabriel would tell me all about Brazil; all the ladies, and how he would go out into the ocean and smoke weed, cops would never follow him in. He has only been in the US for a few months; he learns to speak good English in the time I know him. He is a wild man; he loves to play pool on my patio and talk shit. I kick his ass plenty; he wins sometimes. Never shuts the fuck up, though. I like to talk, but I just have to listen most of the time with him.

He says, "I'm gonna kick your ass on this one, you can't beat me at pool, never, I'm Brazilian. You have no chance, I'm Brazilian."

"Okay, just shoot, fucker."

Every five or ten minutes, he says, "Oh, is that a car? I

got to go." He comes back from valet parking in about ten minutes, and we resume playing the same game.

He would always say, "Eu sei, só—só vá com calma." *I know, just—just take it easy.*

He and I start to play pool every evening. *He even came to visit me later in Colorado. I thought of him as a brother at one point.*

***

Once, Gabriel takes me to a Brazilian club where there are about 100 drums, big ones, small ones, bongos. At one point, the people all walk to their drums and start pounding. I am like, what the hell. It is like a camp meeting revival; everyone starts dancing; I dance my ass off. It is amazing. Those Brazilian girls are so fine.

***

On Saturday, Gabriel and I go with ten other Brazilians to see a reggae music festival at the Los Angeles Memorial Sports Arena. We pile into this big van, and each of us takes a hit of acid. I am in the furthest backseat, listening to all eleven Brazilians speaking Portuguese at the same time. I think, let me out of this fucking van. I love Brazilians, though; they are the coolest people I have ever met. Such happy people.

At the show, I see Burning Speak and Peter Toss, and Ziggy Marley plays too. I get separated from the Brazilians; it's hard tripping on acid when you can't speak the same language. I end up taking the bus home, alone.

***

I had a girlfriend from Brazil when I was living in LA. Her name was Melissa. She was so beautiful, with natural blond hair. She was from Rio de Janeiro. Her dad supposedly had a lot of money. I heard she got married and moved to Minnesota or Wisconsin.

A lot of the other Brazilians don't believe she is Brazilian. I meet her when I am waiting tables for lunch at an old bakery restaurant in Dogtown. The bakery is a landmark. *Though I can't remember the name.* Melissa is the manager. At first, she doesn't like me; she thinks I am sloppy.

At that time, I am not yet homeless, or sleeping in my car. I am staying at a hostel in Santa Monica. There are so many cool people that stay at this hostel, I make a few good friends from Ireland and Britain. We go out most nights for a pint. One night, a Brit and I are walking back to the hostel from the bar, and this crazy guy comes running on the sidewalk and starts throwing punches at us. I am in my black double-breasted suit, and I beat the shit out of him. After I hit him many times and he has blood on his face, he looks up at me and says, "Hit me again." The Brit and I just run away.

Okay, back to Melissa. One of the greatest memories I have in my life is of Melissa and I going down to the Venice boardwalk together; we were going to have lunch. When she picks me up from the hostel in her car, she gets out, runs up to me, and gives me a big kiss. I think, are you kissing me, or am I the one kissing you? Wow. Oh, what a babe. The day is perfect, Melissa is perfect. She is driving wild in her car, and I tell her to slow down, even though I know she wouldn't listen, she just believes she can't be hurt. Melissa is a fantastic woman. We walk down the boardwalk holding hands, there are so many people everywhere.

I see these surfer dudes coming up the boardwalk toward us, holding their boards. When they get close, one of them asks me, "Hey, dude, is that your girlfriend?"

I say, "Yes."

He responds in a perfect Spicoli voice, "You're stoked, dude. You're stoked."

I am so proud. High praise from a surfer on the beauty of my woman is rock fucking solid.

Venice is an acclaimed local surf spot due to the Venice Breakwater that Abbot Kinney built way back in 1905. The first documented surfing demonstration in California was held off Venice Beach by George Freeth in 1907.

Melissa and I go into a little store on the boardwalk to buy some smokes, and as I am paying, she jumps on my back and bites the back of my neck.

I smile big and tell her, "Wait a minute. Take it easy."

She just keeps biting and crawling up my back. I love it. She is exhilarating and crazy good.

Melissa is the one to stay forever in my heart. I will never forget her.

***

Right next to the Sculpture Gardens restaurant and my loft on Abbot Kinney Boulevard is a house that has been owned by a Latino family for decades. I know some of them are cholos in the Venice 13 gang. I get to meet them all. I wouldn't say they are my good friends; they just know me, and I am alright to them. So, it is okay. At first, they call me The Indian, like an American Indian, I guess because I have long hair. One of them is the neighborhood thief; he is a real hustler, his name is Cisco. There is an older brother, Mark, who is disabled. He sleeps in a car, not in the house. He is my best friend from the family, we talk a lot. They have a middle sister who drinks too much and is always shouting. She is really hot tempered. *Once, I had to blast her with a water hose because she was charging me.* At least they don't want to kill me or rob me completely. I find comfort in that. They know I will take no shit.

I have the entire family over for Thanksgiving one time; I make a turkey, stuffing, and everything. Then, when I go home to Colorado for Christmas, they rob me. Swipe my TV, take some CDs, and pull up my pot plant, which isn't even budding yet. Mark ends up bringing back the pot plant, that's how I know it was them. Other than that, they are cool. A couple of months later, they come over to watch the Cowboys in the Super Bowl. We drink so much tequila, I pass out. They have a daughter; she is beautiful, but I never get to talk with her much.

***

A lot of cars are being broken into around Venice Place. The thieves just break out a window and take what they can grab, maybe steal the stereo. The restaurants have started complaining about their customers' property being stolen. Some people start saying they will never come back to eat at Venice Place. I see this as an opportunity to make some extra money as a security guard. I go to all the restaurants and propose that I watch over their customers' cars for $150 each month and a meal when I ask. They all agree. All I have to do is sit out back and make sure no more cars are broken into. When I propose it to the restaurants, I already know who is breaking into the cars. It is Cisco.

So, I go down to the beach and buy a bag of weed, then I go next door and ask for him. I give him the weed and tell him, "You have to stop breaking into cars at Venice Place. I'm the security guard now, so I am responsible. The restaurants know it is you doing the stealing, and I don't want you to get into any trouble with the law." Of course, that is bullshit, but he doesn't know that. Cisco takes the weed and agrees to stop. After that, no other cars are broken into. I continue to get paid by the restaurants for about a year. At night, I go down to Joe's and get the best food in Venice. Wow, I am so smart.

***

One of the great friendships of my life begins at this time with Miguel. He cooks at the Sculpture Gardens and maintains the property of Venice Place. Jerry had told me it is my responsibility to help Miguel with any of the property maintenance. I first meet Miguel when he is a dishwasher at the Sculpture Gardens restaurant. The night he starts, he looks like a deer in headlights, almost fear in his eyes. He came to the USA from Michoacán, Mexico; his family has a farm there. At this time, Miguel doesn't speak any English.

I joke with him, "Proto Mexicano, ondalay, ondalay." He finally smiles. I teach him English, and he teaches me Spanish. It is Miguel and me running the Sculpture Gardens for the lunch shift, one cook and one waiter. It is paradise, like being a waiter in Greece or Italy in a zen garden, a character that lives above a restaurant and waits tables for lunch. I am like Rick from Casablanca—well kind of. *Miguel and I were brothers. We still are even to this day.*

***

One day, Miguel and I go to lunch at this burger joint on Lincoln Boulevard. We are about to enter the front door when this White guy cuts in front of us and goes through, without holding it open for us.

I tell Miguel, "Pinche Gringo."

"Why would a Pinche Gringo, say Pinche Gringo?"

That cracks me up. Miguel has a good sense of humor.

***

Another great friend at the time is Sarah; she is bi-racial, half-Black, half-White. When I meet her, she is about nine months pregnant; she and another woman come in for lunch at the Sculpture Gardens. She orders a glass of wine with her meal.

I tell her, "You shouldn't drink when you're pregnant."

"Oh, I'm only having one glass. They say a little red

wine when you're pregnant is good for the baby."

I can tell she appreciates that I care. We have an immediate bond, she is so cool. Later, she ends up giving birth to a beautiful healthy son.

Once, we are at a large neighborhood party, right in Oakwood, at this house with a big, fenced-in yard in the back. A lot of room. I bet there are about 250 people or more. They have the music bumping, and everyone is dancing. I think I see Bruce for a minute. I might be the only White guy, there are some White women, but no White men. Sarah and I walk out to the front of the house for a minute, and a cop car is driving by. All of a sudden, she just runs and jumps on the hood of the moving cop car. I am shocked. She has no fear, and, to my surprise, the cops like it. I love Sarah. She is crazy fun.

***

A few months after I move into my loft, I meet this brilliant guy from England named Charles. He has a vast knowledge about subjects I don't even know about, and he is crucial to my learning more about the history of life and a greater force. Yet, he is homeless. A socially awkward White guy, right in the middle of the hood. He is like prey for the wolves. I take mercy on him and tell him he can stay in my loft, in the room with the beach scene painted on the walls, if he sands the entire wood floor. He agrees. Somehow, we come up with a hand-held electric sander. We work on the floor for a few days, then we coat the wood with a natural wood wax. This was the beginning of my plan to open an art gallery in that room.

He tells me, "You can never be a great poet unless you are still writing poetry when you are in your 80's."

I reply, "Bullshit, I'm a great poet now."

Charles gives me the book, *I Ching*. A book that, if you are in the right frame of mind, can tell you the future. We do acid, and it is like the book is directly speaking to me. *He signed the book, and I still have it in my bookcase.*

One night, Charles is walking back to the loft, and I hear from the patio my neighbors messing with him down on the street. Cisco and another guy are telling him, "Who the fuck are you, White-boy? Why the fuck are you walking around here? Say something, motherfucker. Don't you hear me talking to you, punk? Say something, bitch."

I see Cisco pushing Charles, so I run down. I have to save him. Cisco might beat him down. "Hey, it's all good, man. I know this guy, he's sanding the floor in my apartment. He's working for me. He's cool; he's with me."

Charles and I walk away quickly. I don't think my neighbors ever mess with Charles again. He finishes up the floor in about a week and does great work. Soon after, he left, I never saw him again.

***

One Saturday, I am helping Miguel with some of the maintenance of the property. As I am walking by the A Votre Santé restaurant in Venice Place, I look in the window, and there is the whole band of the Red Hot Chili Peppers having lunch. Kind of cool. I should have talked to them.

*** *** ***

The Sculpture Gardens has recently hired a new restaurant manager, her name is Michelle. She is beautiful and has recently been divorced. We like each other right off. She is an LA native and has so many stories about growing up there. Many nights, after all the other staff at the Sculpture Gardens have gone home, she and I sit in the restaurant and drink wine. After a while, we go out on a few dates.

Michelle must have been making some good changes because the dinner crowds at the Sculpture Gardens keep getting bigger and bigger. I am raking in the tips. Tonight, we have a packed house; there are five servers working. One of the popular items on the menu is a farm-to-table, delicious, angel hair pasta dish made with tomato, basil, and garlic, all grown fresh in California; adding meat is optional. Jerry shows up to help us out. In the restaurant is this little side room where we make coffees, espressos, and cappuccinos. At first, he tries to do the brews, but he is way too slow. He is just standing right in front of the machine, doing nothing, staring off into space, and we are starting to get all backed up.

I finally have to tell him, "Jerry, you are going to have to move out of the way, or we're not going to be able to keep up. Can you do me a favor and move out of here?"

He kind of gets mad at me, but it is business, we are making money for him, and he is just clogging things up. I tell him I am sorry later that evening. I don't ever want to get on Jerry's bad side.

Two months after she starts, Michelle asks me, "Hey, Mike, my family has a cabin up in Big Bear. Would you like to go up there with me? We both have next weekend off. We could go to a couple of bars I know and go out on the lake. What do you think?"

Big Bear Lake is seven-miles long at an altitude of 6,759 feet. It is in the San Bernardino Mountains, surrounded by the San Bernardino National Forest. There is a small town located along the south shore of the lake, with a population of 5,000 people. I haven't been to any mountains in a long time, so I jump at the opportunity. "Yeah sure, that would be cool. I'd really like to go."

"Good. Okay, then, I will pick you up out front on Saturday at 9:00 am."

We have a great time on the drive up; it takes us a little over two hours. When we get there, we go to the cabin first, then into the little town to go shopping. She wants me to pick out a dress for her. That night, we go out for dinner and drinks. Later, we have a great night sleeping together. She says she wants for us to get up early and go to breakfast and then rent a boat and go out on the lake. The day is June 28, 1992. So we go into this little restaurant; it is a bar, too, and there is a pool table. We sit down and order our breakfast. As we are waiting for our food, I ask her if she wants to play a game of pool. She agrees. We start playing and at 8:05 am, we feel the ground begin to shake, the light over the pool table starts to sway back and forth.

She says, "It's an earthquake."

"Oh, shit. Hey, this isn't so bad. This is kind of cool. So, this is what an earthquake feels like. It's kind of fun."

The 1992 Big Bear earthquake has a magnitude of 6.5; forty percent of the structures in the Big Bear area are damaged, resulting in losses of $60 million; 63 people are injured. *Little did I know that earthquakes weren't fun; the Northridge Earthquake would teach me that later.*

Funny, after the earthquake, we still rent a motorboat and go out on Big Bear Lake. When we get far enough out, Michelle says, "Let's go skinny dipping. You want to?"

"Sure."

She takes off her clothes and dives in. *What a body, I always thought she had one of the best bodies of any girl I ever dated.* I strip down too and dive in. She is wonderful.

We dated for a few months. She told me once when she was meditating, she saw her body rise over her head and was looking down at her. Miguel told me she got married to a rich guy and lives in Brentwood. Good for her, she deserves it.

***

I often walk down to a bar called The Brig at 1515 Abbot Kinney Boulevard. This bar opened in 1952 and is located just down the street from my loft. Bob, the potter, goes there with me sometimes. The mural on the side of the building of The Brig was painted in 1973, depicting Babe and Betty Brandelli, the proprietors at the time. On the sign in front, there is a boxer. Babe is a former Golden Gloves boxer and the bar is full of boxing memorabilia. The place has three pool tables, and some nights, there is live entertainment. There are always cool people at this bar.

I am playing a game of pool one night and kicking ass.

Gabriel is with me. I hear him tell someone, "See, he is Mike Tyson. Boom, boom."

***

A few weeks later, Vino comes to my loft, "Hey, Mike, I got a guy who would like to throw a party in the garden."

"Who is he?"

"He's a big guy in the Crips. Do you have a problem with that?"

"Well, I guess not as long as everything is cool."

"Okay, well, this guy I want you to meet is the leader of the Venice Shoreline Crips. You have to be careful not to say anything wrong."

"Say anything wrong? I'm gonna be me."

"Okay, Mike, can I bring him over?"

"Okay."

A few days later, I hear a knock on my door. It is Vino and this guy. I say, "Hello."

This guy says, "Hey what's up?"

"Well, good to meet you. Vino says you want to throw a party? Would you like a beer?"

So we all have a beer on the patio and talk about having the party in the garden only. By this time, the Sculpture Gardens restaurant has closed and is vacant. I tell him, "We could work it out, we would need to charge a cover, something like that."

We discuss it further, and as he is leaving, he says, "Okay, I'll get back to you, then. Good to meet you."

"Good to meet you, too."

I can tell right off, he is a scary guy. I hear he may have killed a few people, a real trigger puller. On this day, he shows me respect, and I show him respect. We have a great conversation. We drink two beers each.

The Crips never do throw a party at the Sculpture Gardens. I am happy about that, I must say. It is awesome to meet a real gangster, though. The Crips never give me any problem, other than once, and I am a White guy in their neighborhood. *Now, I wasn't hanging out with the Crips, not that I would mind, just that they were a little bit scary.*

***

One night, Bruce and I decide to walk to the Santa Monica Pier for a free concert. The band happens to be Kotoja, a multicultural collaboration between Nigerian and American musicians; we didn't really go because of the band. The concert is great. Everyone is having a wonderful time, there must be one or two thousand people at the show. We meet these two girls and spend the whole time dancing and talking. I think for a minute we might hook up with them. But I somehow get separated and am alone. I look for them for an hour and finally find only Bruce.

When I walk up, he says, "Mike, what the fuck happened to you? We could've gone home with those girls. Damn it, you fucked it up. We could've got some pussy."

"Hey, I looked around, and you all were gone. I've been looking all over for you for the last hour. Damn, they were fine, too."

So, we go buy a couple bottles of Cisco.

As we are walking back on the boardwalk getting closer to my loft, about seven cholos start circling us with their bikes. They must all be in their early to mid-twenties. As they are circling us, they say, "What are you doing, weto? Fuck you, weto."

I am drunk and know we are in trouble. These guys are going to kick our asses. So, I cuss them in Spanish. I know that will get them. I walk straight out of their circling bikes. Behind me, I hear a bike drop to the sidewalk. I just keep walking, I don't even turn around. I hear footsteps running up to me and then, bam, I get hit in the back of the head. Down I go knocked out.

The next thing I remember is waking up with Bruce over me saying, "Mike. Mike. Come on, man, wake up."

"What happened?"

"One of those cholos came up from behind you and hit you in the back of the head."

I grab my chest, "Damn, what did they do?"

"They put their back bike tire on your chest and peeled out a few times."

I am a wreck. They beat me down bad. I can barely walk. So, Bruce helps me to my loft. By the time we get back to Venice Place, I am coming out of it. There are a few of the Mexican cooks out in the garden, I know them all and tell them what has just happened. I joke, "Damn, the cholos beat my ass. You Mexicanos can fight good."

They say, "Pinche loco, Gringo."

So, just to make them believe I am really crazy, I jump into the koi pond which is about four feet deep. I'm just standing in the pond. They shake their heads and laugh. I finally get out, soaking wet, and I walk with Bruce toward the door of my loft. We see Olivia sitting there waiting on my doorstep. Olivia is Bruce's new girlfriend.

Bruce turns to me and asks, "Mike, can me and Olivia sleep out on the patio. After all, I did keep the cholos off you, or I tried to, so they wouldn't kick your ass any more."

I wonder if he really did try to protect me. It's fifty-fifty. Bruce is always working some kind of angle, for only his own benefit. If he has to lie, he doesn't mind. Olivia is homeless, too. She is a White lady, kind of ragged. I feel sorry for her. I hear she might be shooting up in her arm sometimes. So, I say, "Okay, that's cool. Keep it quiet, though, please. Damn, I just need to get to my bed and fall out."

As I finally lay down, Bruce begins to holler at the top of his lungs out on the patio, "Mike's a racist; he hates Latinos. Tonight, he was calling the Mexicans Greasers." Which I didn't. He is directing his diatribe straight to my neighbors. He's going on and on. He says, "Mike's a bad guy. He's a piece of shit. He hates Spanish people."

I lay there for a few minutes, listening to his bullshit, and finally I jump out of bed and run straight out to the patio. I don't say anything, I just grab Bruce and start to beat his ass. I fuck him up. I am tired of his bullshit, and I need him to shut the fuck up. Olivia runs out of my loft and Bruce follows right after her. They both run out fast and very afraid.

The next day, one of my neighbors comes over and says, "Damn, what was all that about last night?"

"Oh, that fucking guy was drunk and lying, so I had to

kick his ass. He's always running his big mouth."

"You like to kick ass, don't you? You were fucking him up last night."

"I don't like to fight, but I will if I have to. He should've shut the fuck up."

A day later, Bruce comes by and stands on Abbott Kinney Boulevard in front of my loft screaming, "Mike, I'm going to fucking kill you. I'm gonna kill you. Nobody puts their motherfucking hands on me and lives. You just wait, Mike. I'm going to get you."

For a few days, I have to look over my shoulder. I mostly stay in my house and keep the door locked. I whipped his ass, but Bruce isn't one to fuck with, I know that. He could kill somebody, he is very capable of doing that. *Eventually, it blew over.*

Rastafari

More and more, my interest in being Rastafari grows. The Rastas are the only people talking about God on Venice Beach. Rastafari is a religious and political movement that started in Jamaica in the 1930s; it combines Protestant Christianity, mysticism, and pan-African political consciousness. Rastas accept a triune God called Jah. Jah has incarnated on Earth several times, including as Jesus Christ and Haile Selassie, Emperor of Ethiopia. Rastas accept much of the Bible, although they believe its message has been corrupted over time by Babylon and western White culture. Rastafari colors are red, gold, and green. Red symbolizes the blood of those killed for the cause of the Black community throughout Jamaican history; gold signifies the wealth of Ethiopia; green represents Jamaica's vegetation and hope for the eradication of suppression.

In Rastafari, Haile Selassie is considered the returned messiah of the Bible, God incarnate. Haile Selassie was born Ras Tafari Makonnen, meaning Lord of Lords, the highest title of lord. He was the emperor of Ethiopia from 1930 to 1974; and a member of the Solomonic dynasty tracing lineage back to Emperor Menelik I, the son of King Solomon and Makeda the Queen of Sheba.

I meet Abdalla one day at the beach. He is a dark-Black Nigerian; he tells me he believes he is a prophet. I feel he is almost a holy man, though he does still believe in that Old Testament kind of vengeful God. Abdalla has a burning fear of God's vengeance coming soon. The Book of Revelations and the day of chastisement is at hand, kind of stuff. We talk about Rastafari all the time.

One day, he and I are sitting in my loft discussing Rastafari, again. He tells me how Jah is everything. The trees, the animals, the air, the wind, the sky, the sun, all humans; even machines are Jah. We are all connected. He knows his Bible, and so do I. I think sometimes I shock him about how much I know. I try to convince him that Love and Jesus do not have anything to do with people dying or being killed. Any blood sacrifice ends with Jesus dying on the cross for our sins. God is not mad at us, and there will not be a huge war to have world peace. After a while, Abdalla begins to admire me and my philosophy. I think he thinks I am a prophet, too.

"Mike, you should be Rastafari."

"I am considering it." I have already bought a book on Rastafari and read the entire thing in just a couple days.

That night, I decide to dread my hair. I get some brown sugar and dissolve it in warm water, then smash my hair together with the mixture. I put it all up in my red-gold-green hat and leave it there for about two weeks. Olivia wove my Rasta hat out of yarn. It is kind of gross to not wash my hair for two weeks, but it works. Soon, I have eleven dreadlocks. These aren't your average skinny and stringy White-guy dreads. No, mine are full and fat. I am now Rastafari. Everything is Jah, all things are intertwined.

***

One night, I am walking up Electric Avenue coming

back from Sarah's apartment, in my red-gold-green hat. I look up and eight Crips are approaching me. I am like, oh shit. This is not good, very dangerous.

"Where's the bud, Rasta?" one asks.

"Man, I wish I knew," I say. "I ain't got none right now."

They pass me. I am so relieved.

***

Abdalla introduces me to one of my best friends, while I am in LA. His name is Chaka, or that is what everyone calls him. He is from Belize, the coolest Dread who is always at peace, it seems. Chaka speaks Spanish and English. When the Mexican cooks sometimes talk shit about us, he tells me later what they were saying. He has a van, which he sleeps in, a self-sufficient, homeless guy. Chaka and I become brothers; he is an inspiration to me. He thinks of me as a leader in the community as I try to champion positive Rasta action and thoughts to Venice Beach. *I hope to see him again one day.*

Abdalla, Chaka, and I go perform on the Third Street Promenade in Santa Monica, one night. Chaka drives us in his van. He brings his guitar; Abdalla and I are the singers. We are planning to sing Bob Marley songs, Abdalla and Chaka know them all. I am still a bit rusty on some of the words, except for one song, *Redemption Song*. When Chaka plays it, I sing to the top of my lungs, "How long shall they kill our prophets, while we stand aside and look, some say it's just a part of it, we got to fulfill the book."

After the song, both Abdalla and Chaka tell me, "Great singing."

We make about $30. Abdalla keeps $20.

***

Another time, Abdalla and I visit his friend in Topanga Canyon. His buddy picks us up, and we go to his house for dinner. I think his name is Joseph; he is a White dude. He has three kids, and his wife is very nice. She cooks a big meal for us, and we all sit and eat together. After we finish, we sing songs and play instruments; they give me the drum. We make a recording of the session.

***

I met Haile Selassie's nephew; someone brought him to my loft. He starts to visit every once in a while. His name is Abraham, he speaks Aramaic. Most visits, he says a prayer for us all in Aramaic. That is the language that Jesus spoke.

Well, one time when he went back to Ethiopia for a visit, he returned with twelve small pins of the Royal Guard of Haile Selassie, the Kebur Zabagna, formed in 1917. He gives me one. I mean, it is an amazing pin, one of a kind. I put it right in the middle of my Coptic cross, which I wear around my neck on a leather string. *I still have the pin and the Coptic cross.*

Haile Selassie's monarchy was formally abolished in March 1975. He died under mysterious circumstances on August 27, 1975. State media reported that Haile Selassie had died of complications from a prostate examination followed up by a prostate operation. His doctor denied that complications had occurred and rejected the government version of his death. The prostate operation in question apparently had taken place months before the state media claimed, and Haile Selassie had apparently enjoyed strong health in his last days. In 1994, an Ethiopian court found several former military officers guilty of strangling the emperor in his bed in 1975.

***

Today, Abdalla and I are walking on Rialto Avenue on our way to the house of someone Abdalla knows. The person isn't home. So, we walk back to my loft and pass this guy out on his porch, we both have on our Rasta hats.

The guy says to Abdalla, "Get your African ass out from in front of my house."

I immediately tell the guy, "Shut the fuck up."

He comes charging off his porch toward us. I'm like what the hell is this guy's problem. He wants to fight Abdalla; I guess he is prejudiced. "If you don't go back up to your porch there's going to be trouble," I say.

"Bring it," the guy says.

"We're going to beat your ass, two on one." That doesn't phase him. After a minute arguing, Abdalla and I just walk away. Prejudice is alive and well in America.

***

Since 1983, every last Sunday in September, on Abbot Kinney Boulevard there has been a street festival called the Abbot Kinney Festival, its motto is All Made in Los Angeles. It is one of the most popular festivals in Southern California. Over the mile-long street, 125,000 people attend the festival every year; there is live music on four stages, 350 vendors, beer gardens, food trucks, booths, and art everywhere. I get the good idea to offer Venice Place parking during the festival; we have 50 parking spaces in a secure lot. Time to bring in the money. I put up signs along the street for $20 parking. I make bank that day.

***

Today, I am on the boardwalk and the comedian Katt Williams—*I think it was him, it might have been Tommy Davidson* —is standing on a wooden box, right in the middle of a large crowd. I stop and listen to some of his jokes.

He says, "Don't give me that shit that weed's a drug. It ain't no motherfuckin' drug. I've done the research. It's just a plant. It just grows like that. And if you just happen to set it on fire, there are some effects." He is very funny.

After he finishes his set, he starts giving out turkeys to everyone. He must have handed out 30 or more turkeys. I am so impressed by this. *He wasn't a big star at that point.*

***

It is drawing close to Christmas, and I am going home to Colorado for a visit with my family. I am going by train.

A couple of days before I am to leave, I go down to the boardwalk and see this young couple. She is about to give birth, probably in the ninth month of her pregnancy. They both have on Rasta hats, and he is trying to grow dreadlocks.

I go up and say, "Hello, how are you guys? I just became Rasta a few months ago." We talk for a while, and then I ask them, "Do you have anywhere to stay for Christmas?"

"No, we don't know where we are staying."

I think, wow this story sounds familiar, kind of like the birth of Jesus story. So, I ask them, "Would you like to stay in my loft while I am away in Colorado?"

Of course, they agree immediately.

They eat Ital and try to live the pure Rastafari way. I am not doing all that; I am still half gangster. They are nice, although he is a bit of a pain. He thinks he is mister righteous. *I remember thinking, just don't preach to me.*

***

On my train trip to Colorado, I have no money to eat. The second day, a family gets on with a big bucket of chicken; it smells so good. I don't have any money, I do have weed though.

So, I walk up and say, "Hello, how are you all today?"

We talk for a while, and then I ask them, "Do you smoke weed?"

They say, "Yes."

We go between the cars and smoke a joint.

When we get back to our seats, they say, "Hey, do you want some chicken?

I say, "Yes."

Got to barter, sometimes.

***

When I return to Venice after Christmas, there are about five Dreads in my house. I tell everyone that they have to go. While I was away, someone stole my charcoal drawing of Bob Marley. That really pisses me off.

I tell Abdalla, "The person who took it will be the one to bring it back."

A few days later, he brings it back and says, "I got it from the one who took it."

Yeah, right. I know he took it. I like the Rastas a lot; just sometimes you have to watch your back around them. Or at least the ones I used to hang out with in Venice.

***

One of my neighbors' boyfriends shows up in this new car.

I tell him, "Man, that's a nice car, dude."

He says, "I stole it."

"You better fucking get rid of it quick, or they're going to bust you."

"No way they'll get me."

Well, he drives around in this stolen car for about a month.

One evening, I am working as the night parking lot security, and Chaka is sitting with me at the table. All of a sudden, a bunch of sirens go off; we look out the gate onto Electric Avenue and see someone speed by in a car and about five cop cars after them. We hear the car go all the way around the block, and then it comes flying through the gate into the Venice Place parking lot, right in front of us. The car crosses the lot and slams into the fence behind my neighbor's house. The guy who stole the car from next door jumps out and starts trying to climb the seven-foot-tall chain link fence. About eight cops have guns drawn on him, and they grab him down. A couple other cops have guns pointing at me and Chaka.

I tell them, "We're security, we're security."

For a minute there, I think the cops might shoot us. They finally haul the guy off.

I told him he was going to get busted.

In-U-Its Loft

The night is finally here, after so much preparation. I am to open a gallery in my loft. It is called In-U-Its Loft. The name doesn't have anything to do with the aborigines, even though I love the Inuits. It really means, In You It's Loft. Charles actually thought up the name. The gallery is a collaboration of twenty artists. All the artists and I have worked hard to get the loft ready. The floor is refinished, there is a seven-foot-tall W-rack set up in the middle of the room with paintings hanging all over it, and the walls are covered with pieces of abstract and Native American art. The patio is set up with a few trees, and a bar with free wine and beer. Many people in Venice know about the opening. A thousand fliers have gone out, all the artists have invited their people, too. One of Jack's friends, Larry, also from Parsons Art School, has painted a 15-foot by 6-foot sign for the patio that reads In-U-Its Loft. We mount the huge sign on a stand and wire a light to shine on it. Larry's girlfriend, Sophia, has been a great help, as well. *I have a painting of hers in my house now.*

A few nights earlier, Jack, Larry, Sophia, Sarah, and I painted the stairs up to my apartment to get the place ready for the gallery opening. We eat some shrooms and paint all the stairs, one stair black, the next stair white. After this, we alternate dipping our hands in black paint and pressing them on the white stairs, then dipping our hands in white paint and pressing them on the black stairs. Every person has a stair with their hands only. It turns out so cool.

As I am preparing the last few things a couple of hours before the opening, I sit on the patio and almost cry. What an amazing thing that I came to LA; what wonderful people are here in California. I love them all.

Then, it is time; all the artists are there, and the first few people show up. It is beautiful, seeing all the artists talking about their pieces of art; it is amazing. Jessica even shows her jewelry in this glass case I got. After an hour, there are about 300 people in my apartment—*well, maybe not that many, close to that, though.*

Jerry comes to the opening. He loves it and has a really good time. He does jump me about the huge sign, though. "You can't put up that sign; it is not up to code."

"Okay, Jerry. I promise, I'll take it down tomorrow."

He says, "Okay, it can stay up tonight."

Peter, the old professor from Santa Monica College who lives down the street from Jessica, comes to the gallery opening. We have a chance to talk, and he tells me he really likes the stairs. He says, "Do you know that hand art is the first form of art ever?"

Sarah tells me to come into the bathroom with her. She locks the door and puts out two lines on the basin; we both have one. Then, she says, "Come on, Michael, let's have sex. Do me right here."

"Are you crazy? There are 300 people out there. Come on, I gotta go. Thank you for asking though. Maybe later." She laughs at me. I laugh back. *I didn't get it on with her though, I remember. Too bad.*

People keep coming up to me, asking for prices. Even Jerry asks for a price. I take the interested party over to the artist of the piece and make an introduction, let the artist sell their own art. *I didn't sell anything that night. I never wanted to sell anything anyway with this gallery. I just wanted to have a huge party for all the artists and for Venice. That's the truth. The opening night of In-U-Its Loft, I was kind of hovering over the floor. It was a great success and one of the best nights of my life.*

***

After the gallery opening, I work with local artists to have featured nights at In-U-Its Loft. I want to get more involved in the community, and I enjoy all the entertainment. So, I set up a schedule of events that happen every month, sometimes every two weeks. I promote the events to the people in Venice.

One of the first events on the schedule is UCLA Film Night. I had visited the UCLA School of Theater, Film and Television and spoken to several students about presenting their short film or documentary. Tonight, we are featuring an animated children's film. A lot of kids with their parents come to the viewing. Everyone is sitting outside in the small amphitheater and enjoying themselves. I also provide free pizza for the guests. Children have never been in my loft, and all the kids running around make it a very happy place.

A couple weeks later, it is Blues & Bar-B-Que Night. I coordinate with a local restaurant, Bar-B-Que Southern Cooking on Abbot Kinney Boulevard. They agree to bring all the food, which is excellent. They have ribs, chicken, hot-links, everything. I get a blues band from the beach to perform. We have about 50 people show up, which is a disappointing turn out. The only people that get paid are the Bar-B-Que people. There isn't even enough money from the cover charge to pay the band, for which they are pissed. Hey, that is the chance they take.

Next is Rastafari Hospitality Night. I coordinate Ital, also spelled I-tal, which is food often celebrated by those in the Rastafari movement. I work with a drum company that brings about twenty drums. There are also African products available for purchase. Many people are playing drums. At one point, Abdalla starts dancing, and everybody joins. It kind of feels like church and being in Africa at the same time. The food is great. The only problem that night is all my Rasta friends have no money, so they came to the event for free. They eat all the food, dance all night, and don't pay a dime. Well, I guess I should have planned for that.

Five days before Thanksgiving is our Turkey Giveaway. I coordinate with a local food bank to provide the turkeys. I get Jack to help me take them down to the boardwalk; we give away twenty turkeys. *Katt Williams gave me that idea.*

Another event cosponsored by In-U-Its Loft is The Firehouse Rave Party. We rent an old firehouse that has been empty for a few years. There is a DJ on an elevated platform, above the dance floor. I also get a great band to perform at the party, White guys with dreadlocks. They kind of sound like the *Red Hot Chili Peppers*. We serve hors d'œuvres, wine, and beer. There are huge draping pieces of art hanging on the walls, each maybe 15 feet tall. It is a pretty big party, many people come, but we are still a little bit disappointed by the turnout.

***

Today, I hear that Roland is out of jail and is somewhere in Venice. I go looking for him. It is Bruce who finally brings him over to my house. It's awesome seeing my friend. All three of us sit on the patio and reminisce on old stories and his time in jail.

Bruce asks us to go over to this abandoned house with him. It is full of people. Bruce buys crack, and Roland and I smoke it with him. *That was the first and only time we had ever done this. Bruce was starting to get on the crack train even then.*

A couple of days later, Roland comes over by himself. We shoot the shit for almost the entire day. As it is getting dark, he asks me, "Don't you have a TV?"

"No. So, if you see one out there, get me one."

"Okay, I will."

The next day, I am told that Roland went to jail again. *That night, he broke into a house and was walking down Pacific Avenue with a TV, probably headed to my house. I never saw him again. So, I guess I got him in trouble again, damn. Well, life goes on.*

***

It is July 28, 1993, and I am off to the movie theater. I hardly ever go to the movies, but I have to see Tupac Shakur and Janet Jackson in *Poetic Justice*. I go by myself. Tupac is so cool, and I love that stud piercing in his nose. I think I have to get one just like it. So, right after the movie, I go straight to the boardwalk to get my nose pierced. I get a stud just like Tupac's. And I add another piercing in my left ear, now I have two. *Let me tell you that nose piercing hurt like shit when they did it.*

Roger Ebert stated, "… Poetic Justice unwinds like a road picture from the early 1970s, in which the characters are introduced and then set off on a trip that becomes a journey of discovery. By the end of the film, Justice will have learned to trust and love again, and Shakur will have learned how to listen to a woman. And all of the characters —who in one way or another lack families—will begin to get a feeling for the larger African/American family to which they belong."

***

A couple months later, I have a busy night scheduled ahead of me. First, I have to go to Jerry's house for a party. Then Shawn—who works at the watch shop—and I are throwing a rave party at the Sculpture Gardens. I get dressed up in my black suit and a silk shirt buttoned to the top with my nice, black, Italian shoes. *I can't remember how I got to Jerry's house in Brentwood, but I was only fashionably late. I think Michelle picked me up and drove me there.* Jerry and Michelle are great friends. We all have time to talk together. Then, I am out. Got to get back to Venice Place. I arrive just as Shawn lets the first people into the Sculpture Gardens. Perfect timing. Jerry doesn't even know I am throwing a party.

Shawn had asked if he could have the party. He and his brother, Terry, invite over 100 people. They are the skater, skateboard crowd, with a few gangster types mixed in. I know there might be a little trouble when they show up with a nitrous oxide tank. Ecstasy is popular with this crowd.

The customers from the restaurants are shocked to see all these characters with their neon necklaces and bracelets partying in the garden. Joe, the owner of Joe's restaurant, comes out and complains, "Hey, Mike, who are all these gangster types around here?"

"Well, they're having a rave party, and it's just for tonight. I will make sure everything goes okay for your customers, that they all get safely to their cars. Okay?"

"Well, okay, if you are going to handle it. Then that's okay."

Shawn and I run a bar with beer and wine and make some good money. At one point, when it is a little slow, I ask him, "Hey, are you good with handling the bar alone for a minute? I want to go out and say hello to your brother."

Shawn says he can handle it. So, I walk to the garden, and Terry is sitting on a table with ten to twelve people standing close around. I see that he is rolling a joint.

"Hey, what's up, Mike? You want a hit?" he asks.

"Yes, of course. What's up with you?"

They all say stuff like, "This party is great. What a wonderful garden. It's a very cool spot. Thank you."

Terry passes me the joint. When I hit it, I immediately know it isn't just weed. I ask, "What is this?"

Everyone starts laughing. "Oh, we put a little crack in with the weed," Terry says.

Wow, I think, why ruin a good joint? I hit it again, tell everyone to have a great time, and go back inside.

Most everybody at the party is pretty cool. However,

the day after the party, Miguel and I have to patch a hole in the wall where someone kicked it in. I am just so happy nothing else was destroyed. *It was a heck of a Rave Party, and no one had anything stolen, at all.*

***

I am settling down for a quiet evening in my loft, and I hear a knock on my door. There is Vino. I have not seen him for a few months. From what I hear, he has come a long way. He is no longer the unkept crackhead he once was. He is clean and looks healthy. Even though Vino has always been a bit of a smart-ass, I like him because of our past. So, tonight, I think it is okay to hang out with him again. We sit in my kitchen and have a beer.

After a couple of beers, he asks, "Hey, Mike, you think you can walk with me over to this place? I need to talk to this guy. It's only a few blocks away."

"Why do you need me to go? Why don't you just go by yourself?"

"You got something better to do, motherfucker?"

"No, and don't call me motherfucker, asshole."

We walk a few blocks to this apartment complex. It is one of those two-story, rectangular buildings, with a big gate at the entrance. As we enter the complex, this huge Black guy standing at the gate puts his hand on my chest. "No White people can come in here," he says.

I stop in my tracks. "Okay."

So, Vino goes in by himself while I stand outside. This is the straight hood. It is a nice night, not too hot, no rain, beautiful California. After about ten minutes, as I am looking up at the stars, Vino comes running out the gate at full speed. There is another Black guy chasing him, followed closely by the big guy from the gate. They run past me into the middle of the four-way intersection. At this point, I see the guy chasing Vino catch him and hit him. Vino falls; the guy has him down on the street and is punching him. I rush over to stop him, and the huge guy from the gate steps in to stop me. I back off, quick; I am not going to fight a giant. So, I am standing there, helplessly, watching my friend get his ass kicked. But I know I cannot stand by and do nothing, even if it costs me my life. *I had learned by that time that life was what you made it; there were worse things than dying.*

So, I scream at the top of my lungs, "PEACE, PEACE, PEACE, PEACE, PEACE…"

I must have said peace about twenty or thirty times before all three of them stop and look at me with amazement and shock, I guess; they have blank stares. They might be a little afraid of me, a crazy man for peace? Finally, the guy who has been hitting Vino walks away from us as fast as he can. The big dude is standing still staring at me as if I have lost my mind. He turns around and quickly goes back into the complex. Vino and I set off fast to my house. He tells me, "Thank you, thank you, thank you, man. You saved my ass. It is like a miracle. Wow. Why the hell did you start yelling peace? You are one crazy motherfucker, Mike."

We get about two blocks away with about two blocks to go, when four police cars roll up on us from all directions. I mean, damn, that is about eight cops.

They tell us, "Get your hands up! Get your hands up! Get up against the wall, now!"

I say, "What? I live here. I live two blocks away. Right up the street. Damn, can't I even walk in my own neighborhood without you guys messing with me? I am just walking down the street, I ain't doing nothing wrong. I live here; this is my neighborhood. I pay rent. What the fuck did you stop me for?"

They all say in unison, "Shut the fuck up and turn around."

I can't believe we are getting hassled by the cops. I am not going to have some racist cops stop my Black friend and me from walking in my own neighborhood. I'm not having it, forget that shit. We haven't done a damn thing wrong. "Don't I still have the right to peaceably walk in my own neighborhood in the United States of America?"

"Shut the fuck up, motherfucker. You ain't shit, you have no rights. We can take you to jail, right now. So, shut the fuck up and keep your hands locked behind your head. No one gives a shit what you have to say." The cops pat us down and have us open our mouths to look inside.

I keep talking, and they continue to tell me to shut the fuck up. I guess they had not planned on a White guy like me totally committed to my Black friend's rights, and mine too. They know if he goes, I go. After a while, they finally get tired of hearing me talk shit and let us go.

They say, "Get the fuck out of here, you piece of shit."

"That's it? You fuckers jack me in my own fucking neighborhood, a tax-paying citizen, and you say hit it? That's it? Isn't there some form of restitution?"

As they get back in their cars, they say, "Get the fuck out of here, punk; you're fucking lucky we don't take you in, smart mouth." They take off.

Now Vino and I are like, what the hell? The fight, then the cops, damn. As we get back to my house, standing in my kitchen, Vino reaches under his tongue and pulls out a couple of crack rocks. He breaks into a huge laugh. "What about that, Mike? Ha, ha, ha."

Even though I want to punch him, we smoke them.

***

My friend Tina works up at the office for the watch shop, above the A Votre Santé restaurant. She is a cool Black lady and not bad looking. She and her friends want to throw a jazz party at the Sculpture Gardens. I say sure. They stop by on Saturday to look at the place. Tina tells me they would like to use the vacant Sculpture Gardens restaurant and garden in the back. I take them on a tour of the property. One of her friends has on this floppy hat. I think, she certainly is fly. They all like the place and are excited to throw the party here.

The night of the jazz party, the entertainment shows up. The piano player is a guy named Rob Mullins. Surprisingly enough, my mom, my sister, my brother, and me paid $20 a ticket in Denver to see him at a place called The Regis Café. Crazy how LA is, he is performing for free at this party. There is also music in the garden, a young woman is featured playing the flute, with a band accompanying her. They are kind of jazz fusion, real cool.

On a few of their songs, the band is playing drums only. For one song, I get up and dance in front of the band and the crowd. It is the best I have ever danced in my life. I am in my double-breasted black suit; I feel like it is my night. After dancing, I am exhausted, so I take a little walk to get some air. At the front gate, there is the girl with the floppy hat. Of course, she doesn't have on her hat tonight. "What are you doing sitting up here at the gate all alone?"

"Someone has to take the money when people come in."

I think, dang, that's pretty cool. Someone having their eye on the ball to make a little cash. We are charging a $10 cover for the party. "What's your name?"

"Lisa."

I can tell right off, she is very nice. We are talking and, out of nowhere, Shawn comes up and tries to cut me out. He is talking to her, and I can't get a word in.

So, finally, I tell him, "Hey, Shawn, we were talking. Can you give us a minute? I would appreciate it." I think I had to ask him twice.

He reluctantly agrees and walks away. I am the king of my domain.

Later, as everyone is having such a good time at the party, here comes Bruce stumbling through the gate, drunk as shit, screaming at the top of his lungs, "Where's Mike? I know fucking Mike; he's my brother. Where's Mike?"

The party immediately comes to attention.

I go up to Bruce, and try to talk to him. He's drunk, so after a few minutes I tell him, "Okay, you got to leave. This is a private party. You can't be here tonight."

"Fuck off."

I ask him several times, but he will not leave. I go up to my loft to deescalate the situation. But I can still hear him hollering, he isn't leaving. So I take off my glasses and go back down to kick him out.

Bruce says, "See, Mike took off his glasses; it's on now."

I grab his arm and try to force him out; he gets off a shot and hits me in the side of the eye. Now, I am pissed. As Bruce and I are struggling, a few men at the party try to help me. Bruce is putting up a pretty good fight and refuses to leave. Eventually, I somehow bend him backwards over a three-foot wrought iron fence, back by the pottery studio. He whines and finally leaves.

Afterward, a big Black guy who tried to help me get Bruce out, comes up to me, "Man, why do you have to be so violent?"

***

Lisa and I start seeing one another after that night. She is a sweetheart. A couple of weeks later, she decides to move in with me. Lisa is beautiful, she has the most beautiful Black skin. Her hair is down to her shoulders, all natural. She has an amazing figure, the most perfect round butt I have ever seen. She was born in Brooklyn, New York, and is a Scorpio like my mom. Her voice sounds like a Jewish lady from Brooklyn, almost like Edith Bunker from *All In The Family*. Her family used to live in a Jewish neighborhood, around Sheepshead Bay. *I was gone, she had me in her hip pocket.*

For a short time, Lisa and I are the happiest people on Earth. It is so nice. We get a kitten we name Princess White Cloud. Lisa works in the day on the Sony Pictures lot; some days she picks up hours in the evening at an Italian restaurant. Every night, she comes home, and we get dinner from one of the restaurants for free, made to order. We frequently listen to Mary J. Blige's album, *What's the 411?* One of our favorite songs is *You Remind Me*: "I seen you before, baby; It's a déjà vu, honey; Don't you know that you remind me?" I definitely feel like I have met Lisa before. We make a great couple.

I meet three of her sisters, they are all living in LA. Her brother-in-law, Vincent, comes over and screens me to make sure it is okay for her to live with me. After our visit he tells Lisa that he approves of me. I like the old-school approach of it all. At first, Lisa thinks my dreads are dirty. I have to show her I wash my hair every day and sometimes put aloe vera on my dreads to moisten them. After a while, she loves my dreads.

The only thing Lisa and I have to worry about are the gunshots going off right outside the property. You quickly get to know the difference between a handgun, shotgun, or machine gun. Sometimes, when it is a machine gun, we duck down, just in case. *It was just a part of living in the hood.*

***

My brother comes by for another visit. This time, he and his wife are to go on a cruise and they stop by to say hello. Lisa and I go with them for a walk on the boardwalk. As we get close to Paloma Avenue, there are two Jewish guys who have set up a table in front of the Shul On The Beach synagogue. They are handing out fliers.

I walk up to the table, take a flier, and start asking them questions. After a few, I ask, "Don't you think there should be a Palestine? What I mean is, don't the Palestinians deserve a country, too? Just like Israel."

"Sure. The Palestinians can have a country any time they want to, it is just that they choose not to. Their leadership is completely corrupt and wants to keep the people under their control."

I vehemently disagree, "Come on, the only reason there isn't a Palestine is because the Israelis won't let the Palestinians have a country. Furthermore, let's face it, the only reason there is a State of Israel, is the same reason there should be a State of Palestine. The UN Partition Plan of Palestine in 1947, made it all possible. Damn, only 22 percent of historic Palestine still remains, in the West Bank, East Jerusalem, and the Gaza Strip." *That got them.* I can tell they are starting to get a little frustrated with me and want me to move on.

Before I walk away, I ask one more question, "Well, do you think Muhammad was a prophet?"

"No."

"That's ridiculous. You just can't have it all your way, that is not going to work. There has to be some compromise and understanding for all religions, not just for one religion. That includes Judaism. Shalom."

My brother has been watching the conversation. He

smiles and walks over to me, "Always trying to start some trouble, hey Mike?"

"You know me. It's just that those guys are all one-sided, the Palestinians need a country, too."

***

In LA, from 1989 to 1993, there were 6,327 drive-by shootings and 9,053 people were shot at. In 1992, the reported number of gang-related homicides in LA County peaked at 803, representing a 77 percent increase over the 1988 figure.

Oakwood, from September 1993 to June 1994, is the most violent; the Venice 13 and the Venice Shoreline Crips declare a gang war. The hostilities marked the peak of gang violence in the history of Los Angeles, a city once labeled the gang capital of the nation. One local newspaper even called the conflict a race war. The United States Postal Service refused to enter the area to deliver mail without police protection. Gunshots outside my windows is a nightly occurrence.

This war left 55 people dead and many more wounded. One of my neighbors, who is only sixteen, gets shot in the arm. The LAPD's Westside anti-gang people say they have never seen so many shootings in such a short time. The war begins, it is said, when a Black woman with ties to the Venice Shoreline Crips shoots and kills a Latino man affiliated with the Venice 13. The woman is killed shortly thereafter. The war directives for the Venice 13 are coming from the Mexican mafia, so as to not share the crack trade.

The Venice 13, founded in the 1950s, are affiliated with the Sureños. The Venice Shoreline Crips were founded in the 1960s, alongside other Crip gangs formed by Tookie Williams and Raymond Washington in South Central.

***

Oakwood is so rough then, that for the first time ever in the history of the Nation of Islam Security Agency (NOISA), the security patrol is fired by the owners of a federally subsidized apartment building on Brooks Avenue. They were ineffective at stemming the drug dealing and other crime there. Alliance Housing Management in LA, manage the privately owned buildings known as Holiday Venice. Initially, the Nation of Islam earned praise for cutting gang crime in 15 low-income buildings in Venice. The unarmed guards clashed regularly with gang members who dealt drugs openly and bullied neighbors. At times, the Nation of Islam sent dozens of suited members to march in formation after confrontations with gangs. The Nation of Islam is a religious and political organization founded by Wallace Fard Muhammad in 1930; Malcolm X joined the organization, after he got out of prison in 1952; Muhammad Ali joined in 1960. In 1965, a year after Malcom X left the Nation of Islam, as he was beginning a speech at the Audubon Ballroom, he was attacked by three gunmen who rushed the stage, firing at him in front of his pregnant wife and three of his daughters, and killing him. He was only 39.

***

Today, my mom and sister are coming to visit me in LA to take a vacation. When I meet them on the street, I have a piercing in my nose, two black, stud earrings in my left ear, and my dreadlocks pulled back in a short ponytail. I am wearing a black beret, and a leather cord with a Coptic cross and a pin of the Royal Guard of Haile Selassie on it hanging around my neck. I have on a Brooklyn Dodgers jersey, baggy black shorts, and high-top Converse Chuck Taylors. The first time they meet Lisa, she has on a white tank top with no bra. *Lisa was always sexy.*

After a few minutes of talking and getting to know Lisa, my mom and sister like her. I take them on a tour of Venice Place. We go to the pottery studio and talk to Bob. Go through the garden. Then we go for a walk to the boardwalk. My mom is a little intimidated, though she enjoys herself. I show them where I used to write poetry.

My sister has rented a convertible, so when we get back, Lisa and I take it for a spin while my mom and sister rest in my loft. I make damn sure to lock the door so no one walks in on them. After our drive, Bruce unfortunately stops by unannounced and meets both of them. Later that afternoon, all of us drive to Hollywood Hills to see the Hollywood sign; then, we get a seafood dinner at Chez Jays at 1657 Ocean Avenue in Santa Monica. My mom and sister sleep in my loft on our futon, and Lisa and I sleep on this huge bean bag in the kitchen. *They were scared all night, thinking it was a very dangerous place.*

My mom, sister, and I have a road trip planned. Lisa has to work, so she can't go with us. We drive up the Pacific Coast Highway from LA to San Francisco and then back home. *I sat in the back; it was one of the best traveling times I ever had in my life.*

First, we visit with my aunt and two of her daughters in Santa Maria. One is about nine months pregnant. We go to a little restaurant for lunch, and this kid just keeps staring at me. I walk outside to have a smoke, and he follows me. "Wow, where are you from?"

"Los Angeles, Venice Beach. You ever been to Venice Beach?"

"No, I haven't. I would like to go, though. I've heard about it." He keeps staring at my hair. "Wow, I like your dreads. They're so cool."

I smile and say thank you. *Along the entire way, people kept coming up and talking to me. It was like I was a super star; it was great.*

After a visit with our relatives, we drive to San Luis Obispo and spend the night. The next day, we tour Hearst Castle, a palace constructed on a hill overlooking the Pacific Ocean near San Simeon. The estate totals more than 250,000 acres and is called La Cuesta Encantada, Spanish for The Enchanted Hill. It was built by William Randolph Hearst between 1919 and 1947. The world's largest private zoo was once located on this estate; there are 127 acres of terraced gardens, fountains, and pools. Hearst's life story is the main inspiration for Charles Foster Kane, the lead character in Orson Welles's film *Citizen Kane* from 1941, which many consider the greatest film ever made.

As we end the tour and are walking outside, the tour guide comes up to me and asks, "Isn't that a Coptic cross?"

"Yes, it is."

We stand there for a few minutes and discuss many subjects: the Coptic cross is also called the Ethiopian cross or Axum cross; King Solomon of ancient Israel and Makeda, the Queen of Sheba, had a son named Menelik; Solomon gave the Ark of the Covenant to Menelik; Menelik took the ark back to Ethiopia; Menelik became the first emperor of Ethiopia and inaugurated the Solomonic dynasty; the Ark of the Covenant is in the ancient holy city of Aksum in Ethiopia, in the Chapel of the Tablet; the relic is entrusted to a single monk for life. The tour guide said that Iyasu the Great, who was Emperor of Ethiopia from 1682 to 1706, and also a member of the Solomonic dynasty, was to have seen and spoken to the Ark of the Covenant in 1691.

Later that day, we drive over the Bixby Creek Bridge, on the Big Sur coast, one of the most photographed bridges in California. We visit a few galleries in Monterey and spend the night in Salinas. We get up early in the morning and head to the Santa Cruz Beach Boardwalk. My mom goes to a beauty salon and gets her hair done. We spend the night in Half Moon Bay, then drive to Burlingame and check in early to a motel, just so we have our lodging covered. We drive up the peninsula to San Francisco and have lunch at Sears Fine Food, which opened in 1938 and is just off Union Square. We go to Coit Tower, a 210-foot tower on Telegraph Hill, and that night, we have dinner in Chinatown at a place called Ton Kiang on Geary Boulevard. They have delicious food, so we have to stand in line to get in. San Francisco's Chinatown is the largest Chinatown outside of Asia as well as the oldest Chinatown in North America.

The next day, we catch the Powell-Hyde cable car to Aquatic Park and go to Fisherman's Wharf for fried clams and Ghirardelli chocolate. Then, we take the San Francisco Bay Cruise, a one-hour ferry cruise that sails past the world-famous sea lions at Pier 39, underneath the Golden Gate Bridge, around Alcatraz Island, past Angel Island State Park, and along the historic waterfront. That night, we have dinner at the Cliff House which overlooks Seal Rocks and provides breathtaking panoramic views of the Pacific Coast since 1863. We sit and watch the sunset over dinner. The next day, we drive back down Pacific Coast Highway to Los Angeles; it takes us a little over nine hours. My mom and sister spend one more night at my loft and get to meet both Chaka and Abdalla. They fly back to Denver in the morning.

***

One day, Lisa and I are walking down Abbot Kinney Boulevard holding hands. We are headed to Pacific Avenue for lunch. As we get close to Brooks Avenue, four young Crips are walking toward us. Lisa quickly lets go of my hand. I think, why did you do that? The Crips pass us by.

***

Again, it is time to run the parking for the Abbot Kinney Street Festival. I am really organized, better than last year. I make way over $500. I have a few t-shirts printed for my company Teach Shirts—positive slogans on t-shirts—I sell them out of the plant booth. Unfortunately, Lisa's nephew rips me off and most of the money is taken.

After the theft, Lisa's sister actually says, "I'll split the money with you."

I told her, "What? It's my money. Okay, if that's how you want it, you keep it all." *Shit, I wasn't going to willingly split my own money.*

***

This night, Lisa is spending the night with her sisters, and I have nothing to do, so I go out walking. I am going past the Twentieth Church of Christ, Scientist located at 132 Brooks Avenue. There are a bunch of stairs up to the front door. I look over, and a few homeless people are sitting there, including Bruce and Big Mary. I haven't seen Big Mary in a while, so I hang out with them. We are passing around a couple of big bottles of Cisco, and Bruce tells me he has some cocaine, so I ask him to give me a snort. He tells me two snorts will cost me twenty bucks. I say okay. After a while, I am getting pretty tweaked and drunk. At one point, I throw one of the empty bottles of Cisco onto Brooks Avenue. It smashes right in the middle of the street. They all start to give me shit and tell me to take it fucking easy; don't get us busted by the cops. Finally, I stumble back to my loft.

A couple of weeks later, Bruce comes to my loft with another Black guy I don't know. I had mistakenly left my door unlocked, and they come walking up the stairs. Bruce is hollering as usual. I am like, oh shit here we go. I have the album *Aja* from Steely Dan playing on the stereo.

When he walks in, he says, "Oh man, I love this music. This is the shit, this used to be the jam back in Miami."

I ask if he wants a drink, and he tells me he does, so I go into the kitchen and make him one. I tell Lisa to stay on this side of the loft with the door closed, and I will get him to leave.

When I come back with the drinks, Bruce says, "You owe me money, Mike. I want it now."

To be truthful, I did owe him the twenty dollars, I had not paid him. I smile, "I don't have any money." I really didn't have any money. *I just smiled to get under his skin, it was probably mean.*

"You're lying, you got some. Give it up."

We argue for a few minutes more, and finally, I say, "Come on, man. I will give it to you tomorrow, at the beach. I will. I just don't have any money on me, right now. So, can you let it go. Okay? And you got to leave now, too. I was doing some things."

I am wearing my black beret, and he smashes the drink glass on my head. At that point, his friend runs out of the loft. We start fighting, and Bruce is getting the better of me, I hate to say. He somehow gets me down on the floor and is on top of me, punching.

Lisa hears the commotion and runs into the room. She sees us fighting, grabs the phone, and starts dialing 911. Bruce notices, gets off of me, and walks toward her. I can take a lot of shit, but I will never let a man hurt my woman, I would rather die than have them hurt a woman. So, I run over to him from behind and right before he gets to Lisa, I put him in a bear hug. He is screaming and flopping, but he can't get away. I walk to the stairs holding him, and he trips me. We go rolling down the full flight of stairs and slam into the door; I am almost knocked out. I want to wring his fucking neck. But, he runs out the door.

Less than a week later, Lisa moves out. "It is just too crazy living here with you in Venice. It scares me."

The possibility of violence in my world was too much for her. I was heartbroken.

***

In November 1993, the Old Topanga Fire starts. It begins north-east of Malibu, near the water tower on Old Topanga Canyon Road. The flames reach up to 200 feet near Saddle Peak. They burn through Carbon Canyon, Rambla Pacifico, Las Flores Canyon, Piedra Gorda, and Pena and Tuna Canyons.

The fire reminds me of the riots, it looks as if the entire city is going to burn down. From my loft, I see the flames on the Santa Monica mountains reaching far up into the sky. It is crazy. The fire ends up killing three and injuring twenty-one others. 16,516 acres are burned, and 388 structures are destroyed.

Several weeks later, the rainy season starts, and the mud off the burn scar begins to flow. Some of the houses on Malibu Beach open their front doors and their back doors and let the mud flow right through to the ocean.

***

Abdalla introduces me to most of the Rastas on the beach. At one point, I think I know every Dread on the boardwalk. They all come over to my house and visit. Word gets around that my place is Rastafari central. At first, some of them ask to crash on the patio or sleep in the beach room for a night. I always graciously try to help. They begin to see me as the leader of the Rastas in Venice. I talk about getting organized and working in the community somehow, to bring talk into action. We need to do something to help others in Venice and maybe even change people's opinions on Rastas for the better.

Abdalla has a new girlfriend, a White girl who has a house in Culver West. He starts showing up in new clothes and riding around in her car. Him being a prophet starts changing, he isn't talking about God much anymore and is quickly becoming Americanized. Chaka and I see the change and think he is a little bit of a fraud. Where did all that religious bravado go? His whole personality changes for the worst. After a while, he isn't even the same guy. Abdalla represented the best of Rastafari, and now he just cares about his own ass. It pisses me off.

Finally, the Rastas take over my loft. There are about eleven living there. They think they own the place. One Rasta asks me, "Why do you always say motherfucker?" I get so sick of everyone, I move into the back house behind Joe's restaurant, above the pottery studio. Chaka sometimes stays out there, too. Neither he nor I can take all the fake Rastas living in my loft. Everyone is pretending to be the most righteous, and they ain't. I am tired of it.

***

This morning, I wake up right before sunrise. The Rastas say First Light, at least Abdalla does. I walk to the beach and along the shore. A black helicopter circles above my head. There is a person pointing a camera at me. I keep walking, and they circle for about five minutes. I go and have breakfast after. It isn't the first time a black helicopter circles above my head in Venice, it happened twice.

***

One night, Chaka is driving Abdalla and me around and, unfortunately, Abdalla and I get into a fight. *I think it was about drugs, he didn't want us to do any.*

So, in the back of the van, he has a hold of my throat, and I have a handful of his dreadlocks. He tells me, "Let go of my dreads."

I say, "Let go of my throat."

I remember telling him, "You don't deserve these dreads." After that, I never saw Abdalla again.

Get Out

This year, I am going to take a flight to Colorado for Christmas. While I am home, my mom convinces me to cut my dreads. I would do most anything to make my mom happy, and she finally wears me down. Besides, the Rastas are beginning to get on my nerves anyway. They talk of being righteous, but I don't see it much in their actions. So, part of me is disenchanted with the Rastas.

When I return to Venice with no dreads, the Rastas say, "How could you do that? How could you cut them? You sold out." They think I betrayed them.

Shortly afterwards, Jerry comes by on his regular Tuesday visit and asks me, "Who are all those guys up in your apartment?"

"They are just some people that I am trying to help out."

"Well, I don't want anybody else up there except you. I want them all out of here. You take care of it, understand?"

"Okay, Jerry, I will tell them to leave."

I actually like what he is saying. Time for the Rastas to go.

So, I go up and tell them, "Okay, everybody has to get going. The owner doesn't want anybody up here, except me. So sorry, but you all have to get your stuff and go."

They look at me as if I have a third eye. Who the hell do I think I am; this is their place, they think. Now, they don't only despise me for cutting my dreads, they also dislike me for kicking them out of my loft. I have become *persona non grata* with the Rastas. To tell you the truth, I don't care anymore; I am not their sponsor.

One of the Rastas tells me, "All you have done for us was just a set-up for the CIA."

What? Kindness without getting anything in return is not a set-up; it is just luck for the receiver. Some of these Dreads are lazy asses and want someone to feed them. I am not their daddy; they are grown men. I am tired of them leaning on me all the time. Even so, I am seen as a traitor to most of them.

One day, about a week after, I hear someone walking up the stairs to my loft. Again, I mistakenly left my door unlocked. It is the Rasta that accused me of being in the CIA. He is half-Rasta and half-gangster, a short, stocky Black guy. He just walks straight past me and Chaka to the patio and grabs the Rasta flag that is still hanging out there.

On his way out, he shouts, "You're a fucking CIA agent. You piece of shit. You're lucky I don't kick your fucking ass, right here."

I say, "Fuck you, man. I took care of you motherfuckers, long enough."

He charges at me and takes a swing, and misses. Somehow, magically, I catch the bottom of his jacket and pull it up over his head, he can't get his arms out. I hit him a few times then push him away.

He is furious. "You're dead. You're dead. I am going to fucking kick you, motherfucker. I'm going to kill you..."

Every time he opens his mouth, I holler back at the top of my lungs, "RASTAFARI, RASTAFARI, RASTAFARI..." I am rebuking his ass with Rastafari. He finally realizes he is not going to be able to talk to me, and he leaves. *I saw him one more time, and he didn't do shit.*

***

After I cut my dreads, I kept them and brought them back to LA with me. When Chaka holds them in his hands, he says, "One day, these dreads will be worth a lot of money."

I still believe in Rastafari and always will; I just don't have dreadlocks on my head.

***

I am walking on Broadway Street through the hood to the Ralph's grocery store on Lincoln Boulevard. I have walked this route so many times before and never have had any problems with the Crips. I guess having long hair or dreads is a way for the Crips to trust me. On this day though, I am a short-hair, White-boy to them. There are about six or seven Crips sitting out on a porch. I look over, and they tell me, "What the fuck you looking at, White-boy? Don't be fucking looking at our house, motherfucker, or we will beat your fucking ass. Get the fuck outta here, bitch."

I don't say anything. I just keep walking. In about a half a block, with the sun to my back, I see a little shadow coming toward me. I move to my right. A bottle comes flying by me. It misses my head by maybe a few feet and smashes onto the street.

I whip around and scream, "Fuck you, motherfuckers.

Fuck you."

I might have short hair, but I am still streetwise. Fuck that. The Crips are all hollering at me, and I think, can I outrun them if they charge? I look down, there is a bottle in the gutter. I pick it up and am ready to throw it at them.

They all start hollering, "Throw it! Throw it!"

It shocks me. They are playing with me. So, I throw the bottle right in the middle of them, at their feet. They all start laughing.

That was how it was in the hood; if they had hit me in the head with the bottle they threw, it was just good fun to them. Also, having a White guy with heart throwing a bottle back at them was so cool. Sometimes, living in the hood was a little dangerous for White guys with short hair.

***

Tonight, Chaka and I are sitting in the back parking lot. I am working security for the restaurants and giving the patrons parking tokens to get out of the lot. It is a beautiful California night. Just perfect. Then, here comes Bruce walking through the gate. He is all beat up with blood on his face. I have fought Bruce a few times by this time, and I am not going to have it again.

He slurs loudly, "Mike, Mike, how you doing?"

Bruce is smoking crack every day, I hear. He is a mess. I immediately get up from my chair and go to my loft. I call 911 and tell them to please send an ambulance. Then I grab a baseball bat and go back to the parking lot.

I walk up to Bruce, who is now sitting in my chair next

to Chaka, and say, "Okay Bruce, you got two ways to go. I already called the ambulance for you. I am going to fuck you up with this bat, and they will take you to the hospital. Or you can leave on your own, right now. So, what's it gonna be?"

He stands up. "Cool it, Mike."

He takes a couple steps toward me, and I raise the bat, ready to swing. He knows, at that moment, I will beat him down. So, thank goodness, he leaves. I would hate to beat someone with a baseball bat. *I only saw Bruce one more time after that, he drove by me in a van when I was walking, hollered out my name, and waved hello.*

***

Today, I am going to each restaurant in Venice Place to sell them the parking tokens. I go into the coffee shop, and the girl that works there starts chewing me out about not having the tokens sooner.

She says, "Where have you been? Our customers needed tokens, and you're nowhere to be found."

"I was really busy, and this was the soonest I could get to it."

She won't take that for an answer and continues to berate me. "I don't care how busy you are, we want tokens when we need them. Our customers are not going to wait on you."

"Okay, if you don't want the tokens, fine with me."

As I begin to leave the shop, this guy, who kind of reminds me of RuPaul, comes running up to me.

I know he works at the coffee shop, and I ask him, "What do you want?"

"Don't you ever talk to her like that."

"Hey, she was the one causing the problem. Not me."

He kicks me in the chest. The guy is about six foot four and wears makeup. It doesn't matter to me that he is gay; why the fuck did he kick me? I charge him. *Let me tell you, he must have been trained, because he proceeded to kick me in the chest about ten times. I think one of the kicks even hit me in the jaw.* That son-of-a-bitch. Eventually, he kicks me all the way outside the coffee shop.

I point my finger at him. "I am going to get you, motherfucker. You can bank on that. I'm gonna fucking get you."

He taunts me, "Anytime, bitch."

My chest hurt for days. I never did get him; in fact, a while after the confrontation, he apologized, and I let it go, even though I wanted to knock him out. C'est la vie.

***

These are some of the hardest times in California for me. The Sculpture Gardens restaurant has long since shut down, the garden is deserted, and not that many people stop by and see me anymore. I start to think I have to get out of LA; I am just about ready to go home to Colorado. Jerry is pushing me to leave, as well. He even has the electricity cut off to my loft. The pressure is mounting from all sides, and I do not know where to turn.

***

On January 17, 1994, in Venice, the Northridge Earthquake brutally wakes me up. The entire Earth begins to shake uncontrollably at 4:31 am. I awake to the ultimate planet rage. I actually jump up and shout out loud, "Oh, God!" *I had been through hell already, I wasn't afraid of anything, but I can honestly say, at that moment, I was terrified.*

The land just shakes with no respect to my thoughts or body. For a minute, I think the entire house is going to collapse, it literally seems to be bouncing up and down; the ground is shaking horizontally and vertically. My pictures are falling off the walls, ceramic vases smash to the floor, dishes are flying out of my kitchen cupboards, my bed is hopping around, beside me. I rush toward my patio door to escape the shaking, and then, I stop. I cannot outrun the shaking Earth. If I am to die today, then, I guess it is time to go. So, I just stand there trying not to fall over. It seems like an immense train is passing right by my body. My life is in the balance, and nature will decide my fate. One of the scariest things with all the shaking is the sound. That's what scares me the most. *It was the loudest sound I had ever heard in my life. It was horrible. In my brain, all I could hear was this loud, evil voice saying, "GET OUT."*

As I am about to lose my mind, the strangest thing happens, the shaking turns into waves. The Earth's crust starts to come in wave after wave. I feel like I am riding a boat. I am so happy the shaking has stopped, the waves are like a saving grace. Finally, the waves pass, as well. *Let me tell you, I was scared shitless. Even though they say that the major shock lasted 20 seconds and registered a magnitude 6.7, to me it seemed like it lasted five minutes.*

I go out on the patio. All the car sirens in the neighborhood are going off. There is no light anywhere, as far as I can see, the sun has not yet risen. People are running out of their homes. Everyone is in utter shock and disbelief.

"That was fucking scary," most are saying.

The earthquake's peak ground velocity is the fastest ever recorded. Two magnitude 6.0 aftershocks follow, the first one minute after the initial event, and the second eleven hours later. There are several thousand smaller aftershocks. The Northridge Earthquake causes $20 billion in damages, plus $40 billion in economic losses, making it the most costly earthquake disaster in USA history. 72 people are killed; 8,700 are injured; 125,000 are displaced. There are 466 fires. 82,000 buildings and 5,400 mobile homes are damaged or destroyed; nine parking structures topple; eleven hospitals suffer structural damage. Three overpasses collapse on the Santa Monica Freeway (I-10), the busiest freeway in the USA; the Golden State Freeway (I-5) collapses and ruptures part of the Antelope Valley Freeway (California 14); the Simi Valley Freeway (California 118) is damaged. An LAPD motorcycle officer plunges to his death after falling 40 feet because of the collapse of the Newhall Pass interchange. The earthquake is named after the San Fernando Valley community; the epicenter is determined to be at Wilbur Avenue and Arminta Street, a mile from the Cal State Northridge campus.

Wow, what a frightful experience. I decide, at that very moment, I am going home to Colorado. No more

California for me. I can take all the gangs, the streets, and everything that comes with it. I just can't take a damn earthquake. I ain't dealing with that shit, fuck that. A lot of people stay, it doesn't seem to bother them, like Miguel. Not me, no way. I like the mountains, where the Earth doesn't shake. Also, I'm not sure I like living on the edge of the Pacific Ocean, either, when it covers 32 percent of the Earth's surface. In my mind, it is almost like the earthquake noise told me to "Get Out." I take it to heart and start making plans to go home.

***

I meet a girl, a few days after, at a little store, when I go to get some smokes. She is sweet, and everyone calls her Angel. She is homeless.

After we have a good chat, I say, "Hey, if you ever need a place to crash, I live over on Abbot Kinney Boulevard. You are more than welcome to sleep on my patio or in a big room that I'm not using."

She says, "Okay, that sounds good."

We walk back to my loft and sit and talk outside some more. She knows about everything. It is amazing how some homeless people are the smartest people in the world. She is, I am so impressed. A few days later, she brings a whole box of books to my house. Books on angels, Buddhism, Hinduism, Jesus, all kinds of cool stuff. I know why everyone calls her Angel. She is an angel. *I felt like God had blessed me in meeting her right before I left California. Although, on the day she brought the books, she also had a guy with her.* He is a White guy, kind of a hick. He has a knife case on his belt. Stringy hair, bad teeth. A little taller than me.

She introduces him. "Mike, this is Ricky."

We talk for a while, and then he abruptly asks, "Hey, I need a place to stay, and I wanted to know if you would rent me a room? Angel said you might."

He doesn't even call me by my name. He probably doesn't even know what my fucking name is. This guy's a clown. Although I do need gas money for the trip to Denver. The little extra money will help. "Well, I am about to move back to Colorado, but until I do, I guess that would be cool. It will cost you $200 a month. Fifty up front."

"Great, I appreciate it. Here's the $50."

A little over a week later, Ricky comes to my loft drunk as shit. He's all pissed off about something. He tells me right off, "You like Angel don't you? I know you do, I see how you look at her. That's my woman, motherfucker. You stay the fuck away from her. You got that?"

"Man, I'm leaving, I'm not trying to find a girlfriend here. I'm gonna be gone."

He slurs, "Yes you are, motherfucker, you're trying to hit on her. I will will fucking cut you."

He opens the belt case and pulls out a knife. With his other hand, he throws one of my chairs across the room, then takes a couple of steps toward me.

I tell him very slowly and calmly, "Hey, come on now. Take it easy. I'm not your enemy. It's going to all be okay, I will be gone real soon. Don't worry. Right now, I'm just going to go take a walk. Okay? You just take it easy here. It's cool. My place is yours."

He lets me leave, thank goodness. It scares me, I don't want to get stabbed in my own place by this dumbshit. After about two hours, I come back, and he is passed out on the floor.

The next morning, he wakes up, and I am there, ready. "Okay, get your shit and get the hell out. I will not have anybody that threatens me stay in my house. Last night was bullshit. Get your shit, or I'm going to call the fucking police. Understand?" *Of course, I never would call the police, but he didn't know that.*

He doesn't say shit. He just packs his stuff and goes. *I never saw him again. Angel didn't come around either.*

***

So many people are trying to leave LA. Of course, I am too. After about a month, I call a big truck rental company to rent a moving truck. They say it would be $1,200 to go to Colorado. Well, I don't have $1,200 just stashed around. So, I ask how much it would be to rent a truck for just a local move. They tell me it requires a $200 deposit to rent the truck, and I need to pay for the mileage. So, I put down the $200 deposit for the local move. When they bring the truck out, I think it looks like the Beverly Hillbillies truck. Oh shit, I'm not going to make it to Colorado in this piece of shit. *It was so old I had to tape down the distributor cap with duct tape in Gallup, NM.*

***

The day I leave Venice, Miguel and I load up my stuff; it almost fills the entire truck. I have so many pieces of art from different artists. I also load up an eight-foot-tall cactus, a big bamboo, and a large tree. I don't know what to do with all of Angel's books, so I decide to take them with me.

It's a sad day; I love California and hate to leave. I'm going to miss Miguel, he is my best friend and brother. Chaka, my brother as well, also stops by; I'm going to miss him, too. We finally have all said our goodbyes, and away I go. As I pass Rose Avenue, I look down the street, and there is Angel riding a bike. Well, I think, she should have come to my house sooner for her books.

***

On the way home to Colorado, I take I-40 East for most of the way and then I-25 North to Denver. I go through Arizona and New Mexico. Right outside of Kingman, Arizona, I see the largest full moon I have ever seen. I pull the truck over and walk out into the desert to smoke a joint. What a wonderful world. I hop back in the truck and start to drive again. I pass by the Hopi Reservation (Hopituskwa). Hopi (peaceful person) live on the First, Second, and Third Mesa. A few miles after the reservation, I hit an awful blizzard, and it eventually ends up ruining some of the plants in the back of the truck. *That was too bad.* The snow is falling so hard, all I can see are the lights of a semi-truck, up ahead of me. I make it though to Gallup, NM and spend the night there.

The next day, I finally get to Denver, I am so elated. I

unload the truck immediately. That night, I take the truck to a local drop-off site. Just so happens, I pull around back, park it, and throw the keys on the floorboard. *You know, I had to leave LA; drastic action was necessary for me to leave California.*

***

My niece is going to be born in April, and I am not going to miss the birth of my sister's first child and Mom's first grandchild. My brother takes a video of the birth. The whole family is there to welcome the first kid in this new generation. I am so happy I made it in time. She is born on April 24, 1994.

***

It's finally spring in Colorado, so my brother and I go camping. We buy a case of beer, some steaks and brats, and go fishing. Tonight, we're in the mountains, sitting around the fire, drinking, and talking. After a few hours, he tells me, "Damn, does everything you say have to have motherfucking in front of it?"

It shocks me. After being in LA so long, I don't even realize that motherfucking isn't an adjective.

***

After being back in Denver for almost a year, I get a call from Lisa. It is strange because I had intentionally set my phone number as unlisted. But I am so happy to hear from her. We speak for an hour, and I try to convince her right off the bat to come to Denver and live with me. After a few more calls, she agrees. She arrives on January 17, 1995; interesting enough, that is the same day, one year before, of the Northridge Earthquake. She takes me out the night after she arrives and buys us a big TV. Within three months of coming to Colorado, Lisa is pregnant. Our son, Michael is born on January 20, 1996.

***

I now live peacefully in Colorado. I never do any drugs, I haven't been in a fight in forever, and my son has never been abused, as I was. Since September 12, 2001, I have meditated twice, every day. I have learned through time that being a good person doesn't have anything to do with someone's religion or certain ideas, it has to do with the love in their heart. I am a follower of Jesus Christ, Buddha, and many others; I love God, Jah, Yahweh, Allah, the Universal Spirit, or whatever name is used. I overcame religion by not being associated with just one. I finally found peace in my soul, my son taught me that.

FOR MORE VISIT
www.michaelruark.com

.

www.ingramcontent.com/pod-product-compliance
Lightning Source LLC
Chambersburg PA
CBHW051827040426
42447CB00006B/407